CENSUS OF INDIA 1911

Census of India 1871-1951, 9 Sets In 384 Bindings (9788121258876) Rs. 700000

Census of India 1911, 23 Vols. In 41 Bindings (9788121271271) Rs. 69000

1. India - Report (9788121275071) Rs. 2475 (Vol. I, Pt. 1)
2. India - Tables (9788121275057) Rs. 2225 (Vol. I, Pt. 2)
3. Andaman and Nicobar Islands - Report & Tables (9788121275033) Rs. 900 (Vol. II, Pt. 1 & 2)
4. Assam - Report (9788121275019) Rs. 1000 (Vol. III, Pt. 1)
5. Assam - Tables (9788121274999) Rs. 1300 (Vol. III, Pt. 2)
6. Baluchistan - Report & Tables (9788121274975) Rs. 950 (Vol. IV, Pt. 1 & 2)
7. Bengal, Bihar And Orissa And Sikkim - Report (9788121274951) Rs. 3100 (Vol. V, Pt. 1)
8. Bengal - Tables (9788121274937) Rs. 2250 (Vol. V, Pt. 2)
9. Bihar And Orissa - Tables and Bengal And Sikkim - Chapter I of Administrative Volume (9788121274913) Rs. 1800 (Vol. V, Pt. 3 & 4)
10. City of Calcutta - Report and Tables and Administrative (9788121274876) Rs. 1300 (Vol. VI, Pt. 1 & 2 & 3)
11. Bombay - Report (9788121274814) Rs. 1950 (Vol. VII, Pt. 1)
12. Bombay - Imperial Tables and Administrative Report (9788121274791) Rs. 3300 (Vol. VII, Pt. 2 & 3)
13. Bombay (Town And Island) - Report And Tables (9788121274753) Rs. 1250 (Vol. VIII, Pt. 1 & 2)
14. Burma - Report (9788121274739) Rs. 2250 (Vol. IX, Pt. 1)
15. Burma - Tables (9788121274715) Rs. 1480 (Vol. IX, Pt. 2)
16. Central Provinces And Berar - Report (9788121274692) Rs. 1475 (Vol. X, Pt. 1)
17. Central Provinces And Berar - Tables (9788121274678) Rs. 1900 (Vol. X, Pt. 2)
18. Coorg - Report And Tables Madras - Report (9788121274630) Rs. 1740 (Vol. XI & Vol. XII, Pt. 1)
19. Madras - Imperial And Provincial Tables (9788121274616) Rs. 1500 (Vol. XII, Pt. 2)
20. Madras - Administrative Report and city of Madras (9788121274593) Rs. 630 (Vol. XII, Pt. 3 & 4)
21. North - West Frontier Province - Report & Tables (9788121274579) Rs. 2150 (Vol. XIII, Pt. 1 & 2)
22. Punjab - Report (9788121274555) Rs. 3000 (Vol. XIV, Pt. 1)
23. Punjab - Tables (9788121274531) Rs. 2200 (Vol. XIV, Pt. 2)
24. Punjab - Appendices To The - Imperial Tables (9788121274517) Rs. 950 (Vol. XIV, Pt. 3)
25. United Provinces of Agra And Oudh - Report (9788121274494) Rs. 2225 (Vol. XV, Pt. 1)
26. United Provinces of Agra And Oudh - Tables (9788121274470) Rs. 4000 (Vol. XV, Pt. 2)
27. United Provinces of Agra And Oudh - Provincial Tables And Appendices (9788121274456) Rs. 570 (Vol. XV, Pt. 3)
28. Baroda - Report (9788121274432) Rs. 2000 (Vol. XVI, Pt. 1)
29. Baroda State - The Imperial Tables (9788121274418) Rs. 850 (Vol. XVI, Pt. 2)
30. Central India Agency - Report And Tables (9788121274395) Rs. 1470 (Vol. XVII)
31. Cochin - Report And Imperial Tables (9788121274371) Rs. 1150 (Vol. XVIII, Pt. 1 & 2)
32. Hyderabad State - Report (9788121274357) Rs. 890 (Vol. XIX, Pt. 1)
33. Hyderabad State - Imperial And Provincial Tables (9788121274333) Rs. 1750 (Vol. XIX, Pt. 2)
34. Kashmir - Report (9788121274319) Rs. 1390 (Vol. XX, Pt. 1)
35. Kashmir - Tables (9788121274296) Rs. 1170 (Vol. XX, Pt. 2)
36. Mysore - Report (9788121274272) Rs. 1200 (Vol. XXI, Pt. 1)
37. Mysore - Tables (9788121274258) Rs. 1500 (Vol. XXI, Pt. 2)
38. Rajputana And Ajmer-Merwara - Report (9788121274234) Rs. 1470 (Vol. XXII, Pt. 1)
39. Rajputana And Ajmer-Merwara - Tables (9788121274210) Rs. 1700 (Vol. XXII, Pt. 2)
40. Travancore - Report (9788121274197) Rs. 1870 (Vol. XXIII, Pt. 1)
41. Travancore - Imperial Tables (9788121274173) Rs. 870 (Vol. XXIII, Pt. 2)

Owing to the antiquity and rarity of this book, certain pages are regrettably absent, and readability is compromised due to the blurring of the original text. If you possess any insights regarding the availability of these missing sections, kindly inform us. Your assistance is crucial in ensuring the completion of this significant work for the benefit of future generations.

CENSUS OF INDIA, 1911

VOLUME - XII

MADRAS

PART III - ADMINISTRATIVE REPORT

PART IV - CITY OF MADRAS

J. CHARTRES MOLONY

GYAN

Published by

Gyan Publishing House
5, Ansari Road
Daryaganj, New Delhi-110002
Phone: 011-47034999, 9811692060
E-mail: books@gyanbooks.com

Distribution Network
gyanbooks.com
India, USA, Canada, UK, Australia

ISBN: 978-81-212-7127-1 (Set) 23 Vols. In 41 Bindings

ISBN: 978-81-212-7459-3 (PB) Vol. XII, Pt. III, IV

First Published, 1912

2nd Impression 2024

Printed at: Gyan Press, Delhi.

CENSUS OF INDIA 1911

CENSUS OF INDIA, 1911.

VOLUME XII.

MADRAS.

PART III.

ADMINISTRATIVE REPORT.

BY

J. CHARTRES MOLONY, I.C.S.,

SUPERINTENDENT OF CENSUS OPERATIONS, MADRAS.

MADRAS:

PRINTED BY THE SUPERINTENDENT, GOVERNMENT PRESS.

1912.

TABLE OF CONTENTS.

THE ADMINISTRATIVE REPORT.

CENSUS OF INDIA, 1911.

MADRAS.

IMPERIAL SERIES, VOLUME XII. PROVINCIAL SERIES, PART III.

ADMINISTRATION OF THE CENSUS.

CHAPTER I.—PRELIMINARY ARRANGEMENTS.

THE results obtained by the taking of the fifth decennial census of the Madras Presidency are set down in Volume XII (Parts I and II) of the Imperial series. The present volume will merely give an account of the procedure by which these results were obtained.

2. I took charge of my office on April 1st, 1910, with an establishment consisting of a personal assistant, a typist, and a peon. As work increased additions were made to this staff, the maximum strength at any time being as follows:—

One personal assistant on Rs. 150 (subsequently raised from November 1st to Rs. 200).
One head clerk on Rs. 60.
One typist-clerk on Rs 30.
One clerk on Rs. 20.
Three peons on Rs. 8 each.
An attender on Rs. 15 was sanctioned, but not employed.

The "personal office," it may be remarked, was always kept distinct from the huge establishments entertained for posting, sorting, and compilation.

3. The actual enumeration of the population is carried out entirely by District officers, assisted by their official establishments, and by volunteer, (or rather unpaid), workers. The first duty of the Census Superintendent is to issue general instructions to each district explaining what he wants to be done. Following the practice of 1901, I issued these instructions in a series of printed circulars, each circular dealing with some definite step towards the end. In some Presidencies printed orders are issued which summarise several steps of the undertaking. The choice between these procedures is a matter for the discretion of the Superintendent; but I imagine that the system hitherto followed is the most suitable for Madras. In many other provinces a Census officer is appointed in each district, whose especial duty it is to see that census work is carried out in his district, and who can expand the summarized instructions of a Census Code, and explain them to his subordinates. In Madras, where such appointment is not feasible, the Collector assumes general responsibility for census work, but amid the press of his daily work he can scarcely be expected to undertake detailed instruction of his subordinates. If then each circular deals exhaustively with the step to which it refers, it is sufficient at first to send to the Collector a supply of printed copies for distribution to all likely to be engaged in census work. I have bound up ten collections of my circulars for the use of my successor; they are undoubtedly long-winded, but I trust that they are clear. For purposes of reference, I have paged this collection consecutively, and references made herein must be read accordingly.

4. The Presidency is already divided into districts, divisions, taluks, and firkas. Much smaller units are needed for the census: a firka may be taken as the starting point and called a charge, charges are divided into circles, and circles into blocks. A "charge" is assigned to a "charge superintendent," who, if possible, should be a permanent Government servant, a "supervisor," attends to a "circle," an "enumerator" to a block. In 1901, Tahsildars were frequently appointed as "charge superintendents." In 1911, Tahsildars superintended all census work in their taluks, but were assigned no definite post.

A block should generally contain about 25 houses, a circle about 500 houses, and a charge as many circles as convenient.

A house is defined as "the dwelling place of one or more families having a separate principal entrance from the common way."

"Common way" does not necessarily mean "highway." A servant's house in the compound of a European bungalow is a separate house, the "common way" here being the compound. A cooly line containing 16 rooms represents 16 houses, if each room has a separate entrance from outside, and does not communicate with its neighbour.

5. There are two methods of arriving at census divisions. One is to call for estimates of the number of houses existing in various villages, form paper divisions on the basis of these estimates, and then check such divisions by actual counting: the other method is to have the actual counting done first, and then form the divisions on the basis of accurate, (or fairly accurate), information.

6. The second method is in my opinion preferable. The village karnam or munsif, from whom estimates connected with a particular village are obtained, has little sense of the value of numbers here: his village, he will say, contains 500 or 1,000 houses; it is pure chance which number he puts down. But, if he actually counts the houses, he cannot go far wrong.

7. This method involves another advantage. The mental digestion of the villager is a slow process; it is well to present to him the idea of census at the earliest possible moment, so that prolonged reflection may ensure his co-operation. The perambulations of the headman on this census quest can scarcely fail to attract notice, whereby the information spreads that some undertaking is forward.

8. When Collectors have been asked to start this counting operation throughout their districts, attention may be given to the preparation of schedule books. A schedule book consists of (1) a cover on which are printed brief instructions and illustrations as to enumeration, (2) sundry schedule pages on which census entries are to be made, and (3) a block list or index to the houses dealt with in such book. Illustrations of (*a*) a block list, (*b*) a schedule page, are appended.

(*a*) *Block List.*

Taluk   **Number and name of $\frac{\text{village}}{\text{ward}}$**

Number of charge.   **Number of circle.**   **Number of block.**

Whether casba or hamlet (in municipalities enter name of street).	Houses.		Families in each house.		Remarks.
	Serial number.	Description, *e.g.*, dwelling-house, temple, shop, chattram, etc.	Serial number.	Name of the head member of each family.	
1	2	3	4	5	6

(b) Schedule.

Name of Taluk
Number of charge
Number of circle
Number and name of village
Number of block
Page

Census number painted on the house.	Serial number of persons enumerated.	Name.	Religion (and sect of Christians).	Male or female.	Married, unmarried or widowed.	Age completed last birth-day.	Caste of Hindus and Jains, tribe or race of those of other religions.	Occupation or means of subsistence of actual workers. Principal occupation.	Occupation or means of subsistence of actual workers. Subsidiary occupation, if any.	If dependent, principal occupation or means of subsistence of actual worker on whom dependent.	District, province or country in which born.	Language ordinarily spoken in the household.	Literate or illiterate.	Whether literate in English.	If the person be insane or totally blind or suffering from corrosive leprosy or both deaf and dumb from birth, enter as such here.
1	2	3	4	5	6	7	8	9	10	11	12	13	14	15	16

9. Sample forms are supplied in English by the Census Commissioner. But details differ for each Presidency, and the first step needed is to see that technical terms quoted, (such as caste names, etc.), are applicable in Madras.

10. The next step is to have these forms translated into the various recognised vernaculars. It is customary to have such work done by the Government Translators, but the elegance of their translations is, as a rule, not understanded of the people. A fair test is to give such translation to an ordinary clerk, and ask him what it means. Generally he does not know; and the literary standard of the composition requires adjustment in confirmity with average intelligence. Grammar is immaterial, and Sanskrit positively objectionable in this connection. When this matter has been settled, forms may be printed up to the requirements of the preceding census, with an addition of (say) 10 *per cent.* to meet natural increase.

11. Leaving the Government Press thus happily occupied, we may return to the districts.

12. The village officer, having counted the houses in his village, sends the result of his labours to the Tahsildar in the following form (house list):—

House List.

District—North Arcot.
Taluk—Vellore.
Language used—Tamil.

Name of * village—Ramapuram.
Survey or paimash number of village—103.
Whether Government, Inam or Zamindari—Government.

(For use outside municipal areas.)

Whether casba or hamlet. If hamlet, enter name of hamlet.	Buildings.				Remarks.	Number of blocks.	Name and occupation of enumerator.	Number of circle.	Name and occupation of supervisor.
	Serial number of all buildings, serial for the village.	Houses ordinarily used as residences.	Buildings not ordinarily used as residences.	Name of principal occupant of occupied houses.		[These columns are not to be filled in by village officers.]			
1	2	3	4	5	6	7	8	9	10
Casba ..	1	1	...	......	Uninhabited.				
	2	1	...	Ramaswami Chetti.	......				
	3	...	1	......	Shop.				
	4	...	1	......	Temple.				
	5	1	...	1. Govinda Medali. 2. Viraswami Mudali.	......				
	6	1	...	......	Choultry.				
	7	1	...	......	Sub-jail. Schedule to be collected.				
	8	... Cart-stand.	1	......	Tahsildar's office.				
	9	1		John Smith.	Household schedule to be collected.				
	10		1	Ahmed Shah, watchman.	School-house.				
	•	•	•	• • •	• • •				
Hamlet-Puttur.	91	1	...	Perumal.	......				
	92	...	1	......	Toddy-shop.				
	•	•	• • •	• • •	• • •				
Total for village and hamlets	143	124	19	......	......				

* *In Malabar substitute* 'désam' *for* 'village.'

13. With the aid of these house lists, and his local knowledge, the Tahsildar divides the sum total of the houses in his taluk into blocks, circles, and charges. In the end considerations as to distance between houses and villages, and the available

supply of competent enumerators determine the sizes of these divisions, but the numbers mentioned in paragraph 4 *supra* are fair working standards.

Statement No. I appended to this chapter gives the number of census divisions formed in the Presidency, and the number of officers assigned to them. It will be noticed that a separate officer was not always available for each division.

14. From the record thus prepared, the Tahsildar writes up an abstract called the *circle list*, one of the most important of all census records. I give its form—

Circle List.

District—Tanjore. Charge No. II.

Taluk—Tanjore. Circle No. 14.

Name and Occupation of Supervisor—A. Ramaswami Aiyangar, Clerk, District Registrar's Office.

Survey or paimash number and name of village.	Whether Government, Inam or Zamindari.	Number of block.	Enumerator's Name.	Enumerator's Occupation.	Numbers of the first and last house included in the block.	Number of houses in the block.	Number of other buildings in the block.	Number of enumeration books required.
1	2	3	4	5	6	7	8	9
113. Muttanúr ...	G.	252	Ranga Reddi	Munsif ...	1— 34	30	4	1
முத்தனூர்.		253	Subramanya Aiyar ..	Monigar ...	35— 67	30	3	1
		254	Viraswami Aiyar ..	Karnam ..	68—103	31	5	1
		255	Shanmugam Pillai .	Ryot ...	104—141	33	5	1
115. Vélúr ...	G.	256	Viraswami Pillai ...	Karnam ...	1— 36	32	4	1
வேலூர்.								
116. Tenpádi ...	I.	257	Krishnaswami Rao ..	Do.	1— 34	30	4	1
தென்பாடி.		258	Venkoba Rao	Ryot ...	35— 65	31	...	1
117. Velángud ...	G.	259	Ramaswami Pillai ...	Karnam ...	1— 40	37	3	1
வெளாங்குடி.								
119. Maraiyúr ...	G.	260 *						
மறையூர்.								
120. Gópléṕádi	G.	261	Rama Mudali ...	Monigar ...	1— 33	30	3	1
கோபால்பாடி.		262	Vira Pillai ...	Karnam ...	34— 67	30	4	1
		263	Ramanuja Aiyangar.	Pral School Master.	68— 91	22	2	1
		264 } †	Krishna Reddi ...	Merchant ...	...	35	...	1
		265 }	Haider Ali Sahib ...	Boat owner...	...	35		1
121. Manalúr ...	Z.	266	Govinda Rao ...	Munsif ..	1— 34	30	4	1
மணலூர்.		267	Srinivasa Aiyar ...	Monigar ...	35— 71	30	7	1
		268	Narayana Pillai ...	Karnam ...	72—105	30	4	1
		269	Khasim Sahib ...	Ryot ...	106—138	30	3	1
		270	Viraswami Chetti ...	Trader ...	139—169	28	3	1
			Railway block No. 17.	......				
						554		18

* Uninhabited.

† These are port blocks. Number of boats which will be enumerated not exactly known, but will be less than 70.

15. Each census appears to present its own peculiar difficulty. The difficulty of 1911 lay in the fact that since 1908 the administrative areas of the Presidency have been changed completely, and the greater part of this change was in progress in 1910. It seemed at first sight a formidable task to create census divisions in non-existent taluks and districts, but in fact the business was not so very difficult. Villages were being transferred in groups from taluk A to taluk B, or groups taken from taluks A and B were combined to form taluk C. Each group affected in taluk A or taluk B was isolated as a charge, and its census superintended by the Tahsildar of taluk A or B as the case might be. The allocation of these charges to their new taluks and districts was done in the Central Abstraction office.

16. Having written up this form (circle list), the Tahsildar checks it on the ground: when it is as correct as he can make it, he has it printed.

Printing appears to me to be necessary. The circle list is needed at every turn by officers engaged in the actual census taking; when the census is taken, it is needed to check the receipt of schedule books sent in to the Central office from the district. The circle list also shows the blocks contained in each village, a piece of information needed for preparation of village statistics. Multiplication of manuscript copies is practically impossible, and one copy has scant chance of surviving the successive handlings of the district and central staff.

In 1901 this printing was done at Collectorate presses, and the expenditure thereon was not debited to census funds. In 1911, seven districts gave out portions of their printing to private presses, at a cost to the Census of Rs. 5,700. A clear understanding on this point should be established in 1921. If all district presses could do the work in 1901, and 18 out of 25 could do it in 1911, all should be able to do it in 1921.

17. Before the circle lists were received in print, I called for a statement from each Tahsildar showing—

(*a*) The number of blocks in his taluk containing under 20 houses.
(*b*) Do. do. 25–29.
(*c*) Do. do. 30 houses and over.

On the basis of this information, I completed the supply of schedule books and despatched them. Books were supplied on the following scale:—

For blocks of 30 houses and over, a book of one cover, 15 schedule leaves, and one block list.

For blocks of 25–29 houses, a book of one cover, twelve schedule leaves, and one block list.

For blocks of 20 houses and under, loose forms at the rate of one cover and one block list per block, and one schedule for every two houses.

18. Books were bound at the Government Press—a plan in my opinion preferable to local binding by enumerators. The enumerator to bind must get, (borrow or steal), a needle and thread, then he leaves out the block list, or puts in half his pages upside down. The Press binds accurately.

19. The supply of forms was ample, but it proved well nigh impossible to get minor officials to understand that one schedule page will easily enumerate 8 persons, and 10 at a pinch. Absolutely preposterous supplemental indents were received from most districts, in many of which loose forms were wasted wholesale. The matter should be dinned into district ears in 1921. If one schedule page will enumerate ten persons, a standard book of 12 leaves (24 pages) will easily suffice for 200 persons. If a taluk contains 180,000 persons, a provision of 9,000 schedule leaves distributed (loose leaves and bound books together) would suffice at a pinch; 12,000 leaves a very respectable margin of safety. There is no meaning in, or excuse for, a supplemental indent of 10,000 leaves.

Statement No. II gives particulars as to the number of forms supplied and used.

20. House lists and similar paper arrangements being complete, the actual numbering of the houses is taken in hand It is a simple business regarding which full details will be found at pages 93–4.

21. *Taking of the census.*—The census is taken in two stages, preliminary and final.

Supposing that an enumerator has to account for 200 persons, it would be well nigh impossible for him to write up particulars for such a number in a single night. Accordingly, each enumerator was directed to commence the round of his block in town on February 4th, and in the country on January 20th. The inmates of the several houses he recorded at whatever rate he pleased, subject only to the proviso that he must complete the work within fifteen days.

The preliminary enumeration was checked by Supervisors and Charge Superintendents as far as possible. It was made on plain paper and when checked was copied into the schedule books provided.

On the night of March 10th, each enumerator went round again with his book, and "called over" the persons entered as dwelling in each house. Those absent were struck out, (unless the absence was merely temporaray and accidental); new comers were written in.

22. *Special arrangements.*--There are certain portions of the Presidency in which the procedure of a preliminary and final census is inapplicable: for example the Agency tracts of Ganjám and Vizagapatam, and the Laccadive Islands. In the Agencies the census was taken piecemeal during a period extending over several days, that of the Laccadives had to be arranged so as to admit of the schedule books reaching the mainland in time for incorporation of provisional totals with those of the rest of the Presidency. In 1901 these island statistics had to be published apart from the others.

No difficulty occurred this year. A full list of all such areas with the method adopted in each case is given at pages 83–92.

All that will be required in 1921 is to send in good time extracts from this list to each Collector, asking him (*a*) whether any additions or deductions have to be made for his district, and (*b*) what procedure he advises in each case. The whole point is to settle the matter in time.

23. *Railways and cantonments.*—The rules for the census of railways and cantonments were passed into law, and communicated to railway and military officers by the Railway Board and Army Department respectively. Unless there is some special reason against it, it would appear preferable to leave the communication of these census rules to the Provincial Superintendent.

To furnish printed copies of general rules to railway and military heads is a simple matter: the point that requires attention is the method adopted to communicate and explain these rules to the numerous subordinates entrusted with their execution. More direct control by the Provincial Superintendent would probably facilitate matters for all concerned.

Under the existing system the railway and military officers make their preliminary arrangements on the basis of general instructions supplied by the Railway Board and the Army Department. These arrangements when complete on paper are sent in to the Provincial Superintendent. In some cases it was found that the misunderstanding of some technical detail at the beginning rendered the completed result quite worthless.

Or in a word the system leaves the Provincial Superintendent little opportunity of knowing what the railway and military officers are doing, or how they have done it, until they announce that their preparations are complete.

24. The rules for railway census are given at length at pages 47–54. The important points may be summarised thus:

(A) Residents in "railway premises" are enumerated in the ordinary method by a railway official, (generally the stationmaster), who is appointed enumerator for the block.

(B) Enumeration of large temporary gangs of workmen employed on railway work, (*e.g.*, repairing a breach), and camping at the site of such work, is undertaken by the officer in charge of such work.

(C) Travellers by rail on the census night. A certain hour for commencement is fixed. In 1911 it was 8 P.M. Enumerators provided with schedule forms and tickets, on which was printed the word "enumerated" in all the vernaculars of the Presidency, were stationed on every platform. Persons arriving at the station with the intention of travelling by any train after 8 P.M. were asked if they had been enumerated at their houses. If they replied in the negative the station enumerator entered them in his schedules, and gave to each person so enumerated a ticket with directions to preserve and show it at the station at which he or she descended.

It is impossible to enumerate in this fashion *all* would-be travellers at large stations, such as the Central Station, Madras, Trichinopoly Fort, Guntakal Junction, etc. Enumerators were therefore kept on duty all through the night at every station throughout this Presidency, who called on each passenger alighting to produce his enumeration ticket. Those arriving without tickets were then enumerated.

It should be remembered that the number of trains running at night through any station in Madras is small; so that the amount of this work at any one station is not really very great.

At some time as near as possible to 6 A.M. on March 11th every running train was stopped at a convenient station, and passengers still unprovided with enumeration tickets were enumerated.

First and second class passengers were provided with schedules which they filled in themselves. These they handed over to the stationmaster, if they left the train before 6 A.M. on March 11th, to the guard, if they were still in the train at that time.

It is essential that the stations included in a *revenue* district should be grouped together as a charge. Railway districts do not always coincide with revenue districts.

25. Rules for the census of cantonments and troops on the march will also be found in the bound volume of circulars (pages 55–61). This census is a simple matter; the only point that needs special attention is the explanation to military enumerators that what is required is *not* the number of men on the rolls of a regiment, but the number of persons actually present within certain limits on the census night.

26. Rules for the enumeration of sea-going population and ports will be found at pages 43–46. This census is carried out by Port officers where such officers exist; in the case of small and unimportant ports temporary arrangements are made by the Collectors of the district.

27. Rules for the enumeration of jails, reformatories and asylums will be found at page 63.

28. Enumeration of travellers by road and houseless poor is best carried out by the police (pages 77–82).

29. *Fairs, festivals, etc.*—Enquiry should be made at an early date in every district as to fairs or festivals likely to attract large crowds to any place on the census night. For these a special staff of enumerators should be appointed, and an ample provision made of loose schedule forms.

30. *Getting in the returns.*—The procedure for districts is described in detail at pages 105–108, that for railways and cantonments at pages 51 and 58. The provisional totals ascertained by the method there described were printed and published on the morning of 17th March, 1911.

31. *Industrial census.*—A description of the steps taken in this connection will be found at pages 97–102. No difficulties arose.

32. *Attitude of the public.*—The people of Madras have now come to understand that the taking of the census does not cover any deep-laid schemes of taxation or decimation. Accordingly, to translate literally their vernacular expression, they "keep quiet."

33. Statement No. III appended to this chapter gives particulars of the expenditure incurred in each district.

34. Although the finance of the census as a whole is treated in Chapter IV, there is a question of expenditure which may be considered at this stage. The question is that of the allowance of travelling expenses to non-official workers.

35. In earlier and more unsophisticated days, work done for the State possessed a glamour that in these more prosaic times has become somewhat dimmed. I doubt if now the ordinary Charge Superintendent or Circle Supervisor attaches much importance to the receipt of a certificate stating that his labours in the cause of the census have been appreciated by the State.

36. An official, for example a Tahsildar or clerk, draws travelling allowance at his ordinary rates when he travels on census duty. But it must be remembered that a district official seldom, if ever, travels on census duty *alone*; such census work as he may do is generally a mere incident in the general purpose of his tour.

37. For non-official Charge Superintendents and Circle Supervisors maximum daily rates of 6 annas, and 4 annas, respectively, were fixed. It is obvious that, in many cases, such payments are quite out of proportion to the expenses actually incurred.

38. Experience has shown that, however carefully the printed circulars referred to at paragraph 3 may be drawn up, difficulties and mis-apprehensions arise, which can best be cleared away by oral explanations and illustrations from some one who has made a special study of the subject.

39. Accordingly, I toured through the Presidency continuously from June to November 1910, holding meetings at several centres in each district, where I met almost all the Charge Superintendents and Circle Supervisors designated for the work. At these meetings every difficulty that had arisen at previous enumerations was illustrated and explained; questions were invited in regard to any complication that local ingenuity could conceive as possible. Illustrations were given as to the methods to be adopted in enumerating lunatics, cranks, *gosha* women, *sanyasis*, and such like fearsome wild-fowl that a census beat invariably starts.

40. These meetings were carefully arranged so as to cause the least possible trouble and expense to those attending. But it is impossible to suit the convenience of every one, and undoubtedly some non-official gentlemen attending these meetings were put to expense for which 4 annas per diem was merely a derisory equivalent. If Superintendents and Supervisors visited the areas assigned to them, and passed on instructions to the village enumerators, (most of them did so), certain further expenses for cart-hire, food, etc., were inevitable. The census being a work of public utility, and one which only occurs at intervals of ten years, it is not unreasonable to expect that well-to-do citizens will lend their assistance, even at a cost, if such cost be to them really a matter of indifference. In very many cases this principle was admitted, and no recompense was claimed for services willingly rendered.

41. But, with all the good-will in the world, there are persons, otherwise well fitted to assist in the census, to whom a pecuniary sacrifice, however small, is not indifferent. Accordingly, I requested every Collector to scrutinize the claims for out-of-pocket expenses sent in to his office, and those, the refusal of which he considered would involve a real hardship, I recommended to Government for payment. The sum total of these recommendations came to about Rs. 2,583.

42. The Census Superintendent of 1921 will probably be confronted with a choice between the following evils:—

(1) Instructions must be given mainly through the medium of circulars; and district conferences restricted to district officials, who must arrange as best as they can for the instruction of non-officials. The objections to this course are, first that the time of a district official is already fully occupied; secondly, that different officials will probably give different solutions of the same difficulties arising in different districts.

(2) Selection of non-officials must be confined to those who are willing and able to give their services gratuitously. I doubt very much if such selection is possible.

(3) A more liberal scale of expenses must be allowed, and the attempt to render each census less costly than its predecessor must be abandoned.

I.—*Census divisions and agency.*

District or State.	Number of			Number of			Average number of occupied houses per		
	Charges.	Circles.	Blocks.	Charge Superintendents.	Supervisors.	Enumerators.	Charge Superintendent.	Supervisor.	Enumerator.
1	2	3	4	5	6	7	8	9	10
Total ...	*1,430*	*16,248*	*348,847*	*1,411*	*15,812*	*302,699*	*5,611*	*501*	*26*
Ganjám	61	795	17,118	61	795	12 590	6,023	462	29
	...	...	*296*	...	...	*189*		..	*32*
Agency, Ganjám	*14*	*121*	*2,656*	*14*	*121*	*469*	*6,159*	*713*	*184*
Vizagapatam	70	984	21.914	70	984	18 991	6,722	478	25
Agency, Vizagapatam	1	8	146	1	7	104	2,889	413	28
	102	*305*	*10,598*	*102*		*305*	*2,143*		*717*
Gódávari	36	539	12,002	36	539	11,734	7,596	507	23
	1	*9*	*228*	*1*	*9*	*177*	*3,596*	*400*	*20*
Agency, Gódávari...	19	91	806	19	91	601	1,292	270	40
	..	.	*1,654*	...	...	*650*	.	..	*25*
Kistna	65	700	15,023	65	697	14,841	5,551	518	24
Guntúr	45	594	12,606	45	594	12,140	7,042	533	26
Nellore	49	525	11,367	49	525	10,754	5,371	501	24
Cuddapah	41	383	8,059	38	379	7,711	4,859	487	24
Kurnool	38	385	8,407	34	383	7,939	5,477	487	23
	4	*11*	*72*	*4*	*11*	*63*	*192*	*70*	*12*
Bellary	40	411	8,370	40	411	7,766	4,601	448	24
Anantapur	46	416	8,408	44	414	7,948	4,320	459	24
Madras	20	113	1,085	20	113	1,085	2,980	627	55
Chingleput	44	449	9,660	44	449	9,312	5,151	505	24
Chittoor	47	454	10,116	47	463	9,428	4,787	496	24
	...	...	*3*	...	...	*2*	...	...	*30*
North Arcot ...	72	577	12,215	69	577	11,657	3,667	438	22
	...	..	*136*	...	...	*42*	...	...	*15*
Salem	46	765	17,367	46	765	12,429	7,539	453	28
	...	...	*116*	...	...	*65*	...	..	*31*
Coimbatore ...	53	884	18,382	53	860	14,795	8,125	501	22
	1	*6*	*442*	*1*	*6*	*315*	*3,006*	*501*	*10*
South Arcot	52	738	15,220	49	738	14,688	7,718	512	26
Tanjore	66	857	18,298	66	858	14,383	6,829	525	31
Trichinopoly ...	48	841	17,371	48	841	15,971	8,618	492	26
	...	*2*	*60*	...	*2*	*44*	...	*623*	*28*
Madura	48	683	14,587	48	683	13,670	7,254	510	25
Rámnád	84	641	15,373	82	641	13,686	3,796	507	24
Tinnevelly	72	989	21,289	71	961	20,218	5,607	414	20
Nilgiris †	18	68	1,435	18	59	944	1,486	440	28
Malabar †	77	1,254	23,163	77	1,196	22,964	6,937	447	23
Laccadive Islands... ...	1	1	11	1	1	11	2,018	2,018	183
Anjengo	2	3	38	2	3	38	471	314	25
South Canara ...	26	426	8,154	24	426	8,031	8,465	453	24
	...	*33*	*882*	...	*33*	*835*		*899*	*24*
Pudukkóttai	17	157	3,316	17	157	2,682	4,504	488	29
Banganapalle	4	21	367	4	21	355	1,915	865	22
Sandúr	1	9	136	1	9	77	2,848	316	38

Note.—Figures in italics are for areas in which a non-synchronous census was taken.

* No Supervisors were appointed.

† Separate statistics for non-synchronous tracts are not available.

II.—*Number of forms supplied and used.*

District or State.	Enumeration book covers (in hundreds).		Block lists (in hundreds).		General Schedules.				Other forms issued.		Remarks.
					Actual number (in hundreds).		Per 100 occupied houses.				
	Supplied.	Used.	Supplied.	Used.	Supplied.	Used.	Supplied.	Used.	House-hold Schedules.	Travellers' tickets (in hundreds).	
1	2	3	4	5	6	7	8	9	10	11	12
Total ...	*3,787*	*3,237*	*3,656*	*3,189*	*43,966*	*38,410*	*56*	*49*	*13,818*	*635*	
Ganjám	155	146	156	147	2,454	2,157	54	47	245	18	
Vizagapatam ...	408	324	242	229	3,631	3,152	52	46	330	20	
Gódávari	163	146	182	148	1,972	1,622	62	51	395	29	
Kistna	169	164	159	158	2,027	1,898	56	53	320	4	
Guntúr	143	127	138	129	1,654	1,468	52	46	160	10	
Nellore	125	116	125	119	1,447	1,162	55	44	95	14	
Cuddapah	134	104	134	109	1,565	1,326	66	56	123	9	Includes Kadiri, Madanapalle and Váyalpad taluks.
Kurnool	93	83	93	85	1,096	948	59	51	120	16	
Bellary	105	85	105	87	1,146	970	62	53	220	20	
Anantapur ...	75	70	75	73	920	871	48	46	150	14	
Madras	17	14	17	17	463	443	78	74	2,000	14	
Chingleput ...	109	96	110	100	1,278	1,125	69	50	720	14	
North Arcot ...	181	140	181	140	2,059	1,954	53	51	120	17	Old district.
Salem	235	144	234	148	2,645	2,339	68	60	431	10	Includes Námakkal and Tiruppattúr taluks.
Coimbatore ...	239	182	229	185	2,713	2,398	63	55	300	14	
South Arcot ...	187	147	187	147	2,178	1,919	53	46	150	31	
Tanjore	201	181	200	192	1,877	1,518	42	34	370	12	
Trichinopoly ...	132	110	132	116	1,567	1,364	38	33	400	8	Includes Karúr taluk.
Madura	164	138	163	140	1,849	1,646	53	47	120	13	
Rámnád ...	152	135	152	135	1,853	1,527	57	47	650	14	
Tinnevelly	200	191	200	194	2,327	2,032	58	51	250	19	
Nilgiris	17	14	17	14	198	165	74	62	1,250	3	
Malabar	265	234	246	232	3,141	2,812	59	52	498	18	
Anjengo	1	1	1	1	5	4	56	50	...	...	
South Canara ...	108	91	107	98	1,168	956	55	45	190	10	
Pudukkóttai ...	37	33	37	24	453	430	59	56	30	4	
Banganapalle ...	4	4	4	4	48	39	63	51	...	2	
Sandúr	1	1	1	1	16	15	58	54	5	2	
South Indian Railway.	21	14	14	9	91	60			2,118	257	
Madras and Southern Mahratta Railway.	12	9	8	5	86	64			2,023	23	
Bengal-Nagpur Railway.	1	1	1	...	7	5	*	*	45	1	* Occupied houses not separately available.
Great Indian Peninsular Railway.	3	2	6	4	35	28			...	...	
Nizam State Railway.	...	...	...	...	2	2			...	...	

III.—District expenditure.

District or State.	Travelling allowance of census officers.	Freight.	Miscellaneous.	Printing charges at Government presses.	Printing charges at Private presses.	Total.	Remarks. (Details of expenses included in column 4.) (a) District office establishment. (b) House numbering. (c) Remuneration of census officers. (d) Local purchase of stationery. (e) Postage. (f) Despatching and other charges.
1	2	3	4	5	6	7	8
	RS.	RS.	RS.	RS.	RS.	RS.	
TOTAL ...	*4,852*	*1,213*	*5,808*	*393*	*5,758*	*18,024*	
Ganjám *	90	163	94	37	...	384	(b) Re. 1; (c) Rs. 93.
Vizagapatam *	111	191	1,756	...	904	2,962	(a) Rs. 482; (b) Rs. 20; (c) Rs. 1,206.
Gódávari *	316	56	171	...	1,535	2,078	(a) Rs. 89; (b) Rs. 16; (d) Rs. 2; (f) Re. 1.
Kistna	119	...	4	...	941	1,064	(f) Rs. 3.
Guntúr	82	21	29	...	429	561	(e) Rs. 25.
Nellore	137	9	...	...	...	146	
Cuddapah	47	...	...	...	...	47	
Kurnool	8	28	...	...	...	36	
Bellary	9	21	4	50	...	84	
Anantapur	118	10	4	...	...	132	(f) Rs. 3.
Madras	1,384	1	3,353	...	293	5,031	(a) Rs. 726; (b) Rs. 115; (c) Rs. 1,108; (d) Rs. 62; (e) Rs. 13.
Chingleput	121	1	...	...	...	122	
Chittoor	20	4	...	...	...	24	
North Arcot	66	17	6	104	...	193	
Salem	239	28	21	...	...	288	
Coimbatore	452	87	...	...	271	810	
South Arcot	39	21	74	...	...	134	(c) Rs. 73.
Tanjore	175	26	4	...	...	205	(f) Re. 1.
Trichinopoly	465	68	18	...	3	554	
Madura	171	110	28	...	590	899	(f) Rs. 22.
Rámnád	171	54	11	...	792	1,028	
Tinnevelly	189	133	...	32	...	354	
Nilgiris	...	...	76	...	...	76	
Malabar	247	103	151	170	...	671	(c) Rs. 120, (f) Rs. 30.
South Canara	76	61	4	...	...	141	

* The figures entered against these districts include charges incurred in their Agency tracts also.

CHAPTER II.—POSTING.

When arrangements are complete for taking the census throughout the Presidency, it is necessary to arrange for a central office or offices at which the work of slip-posting, slip-sorting and compilation of statistics can be carried out.

2. There are five recognized vernaculars in the Presidency: Tamil, Telugu, Malayálam, Canarese and Oriyá. The first two are widespread, the last three are practically confined to Malabar, South Canara, and Ganjám respectively. Comparatively few schedules are filled up in these latter three vernaculars, and men who can decipher them are not easily procurable save in the districts where these languages are in common use. Three mufassal offices have therefore to be established at Calicut, Mangalore and Berhampur.

3. The vast majority of the schedules being filled up in Tamil and Telugu, it was found necessary in 1911, as in 1901, to establish three offices for each of these vernaculars. As in 1901, these six offices were located in Madras. At a later stage, for reasons which will be explained, one of these offices was disbanded.

4. An Abstraction office consists of a Deputy Superintendent with a varying number of "sections." A standard section consists of 21 men whose only needful qualification is ability to read and write a particular vernacular quickly and accurately. To each section are attached a supervisor and three checkers. Record-keepers, attenders, peons, etc., are also required; but full details as to the constitution of the offices in 1911 will be found in G.O. No. 692, Revenue, dated 13th March 1911, and repetition here is therefore needless.

5. The problem that will confront the Superintendent of 1921 will be that of finding accommodation for these large temporary offices.

6. In 1901, the six Tamil and Telugu offices located in Madras were distributed between various bungalows, in different parts of the city. I commenced enquiries for accommodation in good time in 1910, and speedily found that what I wanted was not easily procurable. A full office with ten sections comprises 210 abstractors. Add supervisors, checkers, peons and attenders, allow sufficient space for storage of the schedules, and it will be understood that a building of very considerable dimensions is required. House-owners are not, as a rule, anxious to let dwelling-houses as offices; again a house suitable in every other respect may be useless, if situated far from the heart of the city, where most of the census employees live, and if it is not within convenient distance of a tram line.

7. From my predicament I was rescued by the courtesy of the Army Department, which placed at my disposal the temporarily disused Gun Carriage Factory in Poonamallee Road. This building accommodated with ease six offices, which for a time were much above standard strength; it possesses a water-supply and suitable sanitary accommodation; trams from all quarters of the city run past the gates.

It is practically certain that this building will not be available for census purposes in 1921.

8. The suggestion was made by the Superintendent of 1901 that the Tamil and Telugu offices should be distributed throughout the Presidency. I made enquiries as to the possibilities of Trichinopoly, Rajahmundry, and Bellary, but in none of these places could I find a sufficient office building. It must however be admitted that my enquiries had only commenced when the windfall of the Gun Carriage Factory rendered them superfluous. But I should recommend that the Superintendent of 1921 tackle this problem at least six months before a solution becomes imperative.

At Mangalore, it so happened that the jail had been given up and the building was vacant. The Inspector-General of Prisons kindly placed this at my disposal. The building may not be available in 1921 but, as four sections suffice for Canarese work, it is not likely that any serious difficulty will be experienced.

At Calicut, where the Malayálam work was done by six sections, I rented a very fair house on the sea front for Rs. 100 per mensem. As illustrating the increase in the cost of everything, I may mention that in 1901 a building (now used as a Post office) large enough to accommodate the Malayálam and Canarese offices was secured for Rs. 70 per mensem.

At Berhampur, in 1901, a disused building (Military hospital and office buildings) was available. In 1911, I had to pay Rs. 60 per mensem for very inferior accommodation in the centre of the town.

9. *Furniture.*—When suitable buildings are obtained, they must be furnished. Whatever be the case elsewhere, it is certain that the modern Madrasi has lost the art of writing while sitting on the floor. He can do it for a time perhaps, but he soon becomes cramped and sleepy. Any saving effected by denying him a chair, I take it, is more than counterbalanced by the falling-off in his work.

Owing to changes in the dates of University and Government examinations, it was no longer possible to borrow all the furniture required from the University, the Commissioner for Government Examinations and various educational institutions. Yet all officers to whom I applied aided me to the best of their power, and to all my thanks are due. The following table shows the extent of my borrowings:—

Commissioner for Government Examinations	600 tables.	300 stools.
University of Madras	935 ,,	935 chairs.
Presidency College	101 ,,	73 ,, and 16 benches.
Law College		28 benches.

To supplement this, I purchased chairs and tables from the bazaar and Messrs. Dymes & Co., at a total cost of Rs. 1,514. These I subsequently sold for Rs. 573.

The mufassal offices were supplied as follows:—

Office.	Purchased.				Borrowed.		Cost.
	Chairs.	Tables.	Record racks.	Sorting racks.	Chairs.	Tables.	
							Rs.
Calicut	60	39	...	120	89	105	214
Mangalore	99	99	2	80	...	...	449
Berhampur	75	75	6	60	...	...	470

10. The next essential is a sorting rack for each worker. This is a set of thirty pigeon holes.

15″ (width); 21″ (height)

Others male unmarried.	Animistic male unmarried.	Christian male unmarried.	Musalman male unmarried.	Hindu male unmarried.
Others male married.	Animistic male married.	Christian male married.	Musalman male married.	Hindu male married.
Others male widowed.	Animistic male widowed.	Christian male widowed.	Musalman male widowed.	Hindu male widowed.
Others female unmarried.	Animistic female unmarried.	Christian female unmarried.	Musalman female unmarried.	Hindu female unmarried.
Others female married.	Animistic female married.	Christian female married.	Musalman female married.	Hindu female married.
Others female widowed.	Animistic female widowed.	Christian female widowed.	Musalman female widowed.	Hindu female widowed.

The entries "Hindu male unmarried," etc., show the order in which blank slips were placed in these pigeon holes. This order is learned in a few minutes, and a poster's hand soon goes automatically to the sort of slip he requires.

For Madras I purchased 1,600 of these; made in tin at Rs. 87-8-0 per 100; for the mufassal offices, where tin was not available, these were made in wood at the following rates:—

	RS.	A.	P.
Mangalore	1	12	0
Calicut	1	0	0
Berhampur	2	8	0

Tin racks, though light, are bulky and fragile: thus, although their prime cost in Madras is much lower than that of the wooden racks made in the mufassal, railway charges and damage in transit make it uneconomical to supply the mufassal offices from Madras.

11. Racks on which to keep schedule books are required. I found 24 fine racks at the Gun Carriage Factory: in addition I borrowed from—

Chief Secretariat	8
Board of Revenue (Land Revenue)	3
Do. (Settlement)	1
Conservator of Forests, Central Circle	4

12. Boxes on which to pack posted slips are required. They were procured as follows:—

Purchased in the market	50
Obtained through Stationery Superintendent	269

13. *Equipment.*—Pens, pencils, ink, string, India rubber, etc., are all needed. The following table shows the supply and expenditure:—

Name of article.	Receipt.	Expenditure.	Name of article.	Receipt.	Expenditure.
Paper, printing, double foolscap. Reams.	45	45	Rubber piece ... ... No.	1,440	1,404
Note paper, crown vellum ... "	13	13	Penholders ... ... "	860	860
Note paper covers, crown vellum. No.	2,000	2,000	Scissors (large) ... ... "	12	10
Paper, brown, cartridge ... Reams.	17	17	Needle ... ... "	248	200
Paper, cream-wove, Europe, 15 lb. "	15	15	Pins (of all sizes) ... Sheets.	225	225
			Punch pillers ... ... No	12	7
Badami paper ... ... "	7	7	Red sealing wax (country) ... Lb.	4	4
Double foolscap printing paper, 16 lb. "	19	19	Red sealing wax (Europe) ... "	2	2
			Longcloth ... ... Yds.	5	5
Carbon paper ... ... "	1	1	Salampore cloth (blue) ... "	200	200
Manifolding paper ... ... "	4	4	Wax cloth ... ... "	10	10
Stencil paper for cyclostyle ... Quires.	12	12	White tape (country) ... ... Rolls.	250	200
Paper, blotting ... ... Reams.	6	6	White tape (Europe) ... ... Pieces.	50	50
Black ink powder ... ... Packets.	250	31	Cotton thread, twisted, coloured. Lb.	1,000	950
Blue black ink ... ... Jars.	10	10			
Red ink powder ... ... Oz.	60	36	Tape-tags No.	12,000	12,000
Blackwood's red ink ... ... Jars.	6	6	Country twine ... ... Lb.	250	238
Inkstand, wooden, flat ... ... No.	12	*5	Ribbon ... ... No.	6	6
Inkstand, wooden boxes ... "	144	*44	Eraser for type-writer ... Pieces.	3	3
Ink glasses for wooden ink-stands. "	24	*8	Hone and strop ... ... Each.	6	* 5
			Round rulers ... ... No.	100	* 80
Wooden flats with lead ... ... "	36	11	Straw boards ... ... "	830	830
Pencils, blacklead, ordinary ... Gross.	230	230	Gum ... ... Lb.	75	70
Ink for cyclostyle ... ... 8 tola tins.	15	15	Dindigul padlocks ... ... No.	50	*30
			Locks, common ... ... "	160	† 160
Blue pencils ... ... No.	720	220	Brass paper fastener ... Gross.	16	16
Red pencils ... ... No.	60	60	Penknives ... ... No.	152	* 109
Steel nibs ... ... Gross.	70	68	Ink bottles, earthenware ... "	500	† 500

* The remainder was returned to Stationery office after use. † Purchased locally.

14. *Arrival of the schedules.*—When but one office exists in a town, the Deputy Superintendent can arrange for the receipt and arrangement of schedules sent to his address. When six offices are located in one place, as in Madras, and schedules

arrive by the ton at different railway stations, it is best to arrange with a contractor for their collection and delivery. This duty was carried out in 1901 and 1911 by Messrs. G. Ramaswami Nayudu & Sons, railway contractors.

As the schedules arrive, the bundles must be opened by the record-keeper and his assistants, and the contents checked carefully with the circle lists to see that no books are missing. They are then arranged in racks by circles, charges, taluks and districts.

15. *Slip-posting and sorting.*—I have had bound for the use of my successor ten sets of the rules followed in 1911. Most of these I inherited from Mr. Francis, the Superintendent of 1901, who observed very justly in his administration report that these rules, which are almost incomprehensible when read straight through, become very simple when seen step by step in actual operation. I shall therefore merely indicate the steps followed by me to gain an insight into the working.

16. *Posting.*—The entries found in a schedule against each person are posted on a separate slip. The following illustration shows a slip. The numbering of the columns corresponds to that of the columns of the schedule.

No.

7.

8.

9.

10.

11.

12.

13.

14.

15.

I would add one more column at the top of this slip for the name of the taluk to which the person enumerated belongs. As will be explained hereafter the taluk is the sorting unit, and in 1911 either through carelessness, or sometimes, I fear, through the malice of sorters, slips for different units were mixed up. If each slip bears the name of the unit to which it refers, such mistakes are impossible or at least very easily rectified.

17. The *colour* of a slip shows the religion of the person to whom it refers. Hindus (the most numerous community) were posted on brown slips (unbleached badami), Muhammadans on blue slips, Christians on red, Jains on yellow, Animists on green, others on white.

18. Sex and civil condition were distinguished thus :—

Unmarried. Married. Widowed.

Male ... ...

Female ... ...

In 1901 civil conditions were distinguished by varying sizes of slip, while difference of sex was indicated by cutting off the right-hand top corner of female slips. This method of distinction appears preferable to that of 1911 ; especially at the sorting stage when it makes wrong grouping of slips impossible.

19. Cutting all slips of uniform size and making distinctions by symbols render he work of cutting easier for the Press. It allows also a certain economy of

paper, although this proved to be not so great as had been expected, as unmarried and widowed slips cannot be cut too closely for fear of cutting off the projecting ends of the symbol.

20. The following statement shows—

(*a*) The amount of paper of each sort procured for slips ;
(*b*) The amount cut up ; and
(*c*) The number of slips of each sort cut from a standard sheet.

—	Paper obtained from		Male slips (000's omitted).			Female slips (000's omitted.)			Quantity cut.
	Calcutta.	Stationery office.	Unmarried.	Married.	Widowed.	Unmarried.	Married.	Widowed.	
	Reams.	Reams.							Reams.
Badami (Hindu.)	(*a*) 2,000	(*c*) 150	11,516	8,430	993	8,120	8,874	4,098	2,117
Blue (Musalman.)	(*b*) 58	(*d*) 5	900	589	64	683	638	284	61½
Red (Christian.)	(*b*) 25	(*d*) 10½	363	263	34	323	278	106	31
Green (Animistic.)	(*b*) 16	...	213	164	18	173	164	54	15
Deep Yellow (Jain.)	(*b*) 1	...	11	9	3	7	9	7	1

(*a*) Forty-four married and 40 unmarried and widowed slips each standard sheet.
(*b*) One hundred and eight slips each standard sheet.
(*c*) Forty slips each standard sheet.
(*d*) Forty-eight slips each standard sheet.

21. The civil condition of a Hindu can ordinarily be distinguished by his or her appearance. An ingenious method of distinction was adopted in Mysore, where small *sketches* were printed on each slip. Bachelorhood for males was indicated by a school boy, marriage by a middle-aged turbaned man, widowhood by an old man without a turban. For women the figures were those of a young girl without a *táli*, a married woman with a *táli* and spot on her forehead, a widow in widow's weeds with a shaven head. The idea is far more obvious to posters and sorters than that conveyed by arbitrary symbols.

22. The secret of quick slip-posting is the invention of intelligible abbreviations. The best known of these is the "two tick" abbreviation. Each district has a recognized vernacular : if a person born in each district returns the recognized vernacular language as his or her mother-tongue, columns 12 and 13 on the slip are filled in with ticks (✓).

23. The predominant castes in each district can be ascertained by a reference to previous census tables. For the most numerous castes abbreviations can be invented.

24. Some 75 per cent. of the population of the Presidency follow agricultural occupations, such as (*a*) cultivating landlord, (*b*) non-cultivating landlord, (*c*) cultivating tenant, (*d*) non-cultivating tenant, (*e*) farm labourer. Abbreviations for such are easy matter.

25. The population is divided into literates and illiterates—a distinction which can easily be shown.

5

26. The following illustration shows a slip containing every possible abbreviation :—

No. 12-86-3.
7. 36.
8. Vel.
9. N.C.L
10. Village Munsif.
11.
12. ✓
13. ✓
14. Lit.
15. E.

27. The meanings of these abbreviations are as follows:—

The small black square shows that the person referred to is a *married man.*

Of the numbers in the first line, the first is the *charge* number, the second is the *block* number, the third is the person's *serial number on the schedule book.*

His age is 36.

By caste he is a Vellála.

His principal occupation is that of *non-cultivating landlord*; his secondary occupation that of *village munsif.*

As he is a worker, column 11 of the schedule has been left blank.

The ticks in columns 12 and 13 show that he was born in the district which is being posted, and that he speaks the recognized vernacular of that district.

He is *literate*; and the last column shows that he is *literate in English.*

The entries on this slip are in English, but vernacular equivalents are not difficult. They can be made arbitrarily, the only necessity being that all posters engaged should use the same abbreviation to express the same meaning.

28. Before the census was actually taken, the Deputy Superintendents, Supervisors, and checkers, of all nine offices, had been appointed. Many of these were taking an actual part in the district work. Allowing, therefore, ten days from the census night, I assembled all Deputy Superintendents and Supervisors at the Gun Carriage Factory on March 20th. There we took up three divisions of Madras City, containing 86,500 inhabitants, the entries for whom were made in English, and were therefore intelligible to all these officials, many of whom had no Indian language in common.

Slips were posted for these divisions and sorted for all tables except XV (occupations). Supervisors worked as posting and sorting clerks, Deputy Superintendents, as Supervisors. Four of the Deputy Superintendents, and my Personal Assistant had been engaged in some capacity in this work in 1901; and their experience proved most valuable. No attempt was made to attain a very high rate of speed, but by April 1st, when this experimental office closed, we had all attained a fair working knowledge of how the thing should be done. In the light of experience thus gained, the rules of 1901 were re-drafted and printed.

29. Mufassal Deputy Superintendents went to their stations, assembled their sorters, and started work. Four of the Madras offices opened on April 3rd, though not at full strength. The remaining two opened three weeks later, their Deputy Superintendents and Supervisors having been engaged meanwhile in selecting men for appointment as posters, and assisting the record-keeper in check and arrangement of the huge masses of schedules received from the Telugu and Tamil districts. The following statement shows the progress of all offices to full strength.

Office number.	Date when it was opened.	Number of sections with which opened.	Date when sections were added.	Number of sections added.	Date when sections were added.	Number of sections added.	Date when sections were complete.	Total number of sections.
I	3rd Apl. 1911	5	17th Apl. 1911	5	...	...	17th Apl. 1911	10
II	3rd " "	4	5th " "	3	17th Apl. 1911 8th May "	3 1	8th May "	11
III	24th " "	5	1st May "	5	16th " "	1	1st " "	11
IV	3rd " "	8	27th Apl. "	1	3rd " "	1	3rd " "	10
V	24th " "	6	1st May "	5	......	...	1st " "	11
VI	3rd " "	5	21st Apl. "	5	......	...	21st Apl. "	10
VII (Calicut) ...	5th " "	6	......	...	......	...	5th " "	6
VIII (Mangalore).	5th " "	4	......	...	......	...	5th " "	4
IX (Berhampur).	5th " "	3	......	...	......	...	5th " "	3
						Total number of sections ...		76

30. The following statement shows the time occupied in posting by each office, the average speed attained during the first and last weeks, the general average of all offices, and the maximum number posted on any day by one man in each office :—

Office number.	Number of sections.	Maximum number of clerks in a section.	Population dealt with.	Date when posting commenced.	Date when posting finished.	Average posted for first week.	Average posted for last week.	Average posted when the office was in full swing.	General average for all offices.	Highest number posted by any man.
I ...	10	25	7,230,488	3rd Apl. 1911	12th June 1911	462	721	728	756	1,524
II ...	11	25	6,725,918	3rd " "	14th " "	420	749	784		1,534
III ...	11	25	6,549,592	24th " "	17th " "	455	707	756		1,504
IV ...	10	25	5,293,341	3rd " "	2nd " "	441	777	777		1,560
V ...	11	25	3,815,405	24th " "	8th " "	469	756	728		1,419
VI ...	10	25	6,176,058	3rd " "	6th " "	448	672	833		1,737
VII ...	6	20	3,111,343	5th " "	23rd May "	392	812	812		1,642
VIII ...	4	20	1,595,675*	5th " "	19th " "	385	707	707		1,227
IX ...	3	21	1,541,316	5th " "	2nd June "	Not given.	826	826		1,301

* Includes Coorg.

31. The next statement shows the total number copied in each week and the number of slips checked The gradual falling off towards the end is due to the fact that some offices had finished posting, and commenced sorting, earlier than others.

Week ending.	Number of slips copied.	NUMBER OF SLIPS CHECKED BY			Number of errors found by all officers.
		Checkers.	Supervisors.	Deputy Superintendents.	
8th April 1911 ...	1,268,511	256,530	37,762	12,598	3,963
15th " " ...	1,326,486	437,410	73,737	12,522	5,856
22nd " " ...	3,428,251	1,011,582	131,572	28,296	8,306
29th " " ...	4,360,434	1,413,524	156,514	28,934	8,395
6th May 1911 ...	5,163,804	1,724,268	172,614	19,725	10,602
13th " " ...	6,076,262	2,070,281	207,441	19,839	11,772
20th " " ...	6,752,891	2,488,137	224,162	18,494	13,819
27th " " ...	5,677,671	2,306,663	162,339	9,105	11,306
3rd June 1911 ...	3,866,500	1,505,372	95,309	7,846	6,431
10th " " ...	3,223,225	1,219,589	78,733	5,205	5,718
17th " " ...	718,230	287,890	26,980	240	900
	41,761,745	14,721,246	1,367,153	162,304	87,063
Percentage on total number copied.	....	35·3	3·3	0·38	0·21

32. *Payment.*—During the month of May As. 8 were paid for 500 correctly posted slips. After May, the rate was raised to 8 annas for 600 slips.

33. *Posting of infirmities.*—Entries of infirmities are comparatively few, and are scattered throughout a multitude of books. The simplest method is to disregard them at first, and, when all the books have been posted for an office, to re-post on separate slips all persons suffering from any infirmity. These slips are kept separate, and are separately sorted. Care should be taken not to add their total to the general total in which they have already been included. Posters were paid at a fixed rate of As. 8 per day while engaged on this work.

The following statement shows the amount paid in each office to posters only for posting and infirmity posting combined :—

Office number.	Amount paid to Posters. Rs.
I	6,981
II	7,131
III	5,832
IV	5,464
V	3,954
VI	5,767
VII	2,916
VIII	1,666
IX	1,562

34. Schedule books are issued talukwar to a section. When all books have been posted and slips checked, slips are tied up by blocks and circles, and are packed in the dealwood boxes referred to in paragraph 12. The books are returned to the record-room, and the packed boxes stored in some convenient place.

35. It is of the utmost importance that checking should keep pace as nearly as possible with posting, and that the books for a taluk should go back to the record-room, and the posted slips be securely packed, before books for another taluk are issued. Otherwise an office becomes choked up with schedule books and boxes.

CHAPTER III.—SORTING AND COMPILATION.

WHEN particulars for every person entered in a schedule book have been transferred to a slip in the manner already described, these slips are sorted into various combinations, (sex, religion, age, caste, etc., etc.), and counted. The totals thus ascertained are entered in the forms prescribed for the various tables, when printing and publication only remain.

2. But sorting is hardly so simple an operation as the above description might imply. It is undertaken with certain general principles in view, and carried out under a good many detailed regulations.

3. For the due ordering of the matter in 1911, fairly elaborate and precise rules were drawn up; they will be found at pages 26 *et seq.* of the volume of Posting and Sorting rules which I am leaving for my successor. Read without practical illustration they are well nigh unintelligible; in actual operation they explain themselves. In the following remarks I shall endeavour to give an account, intelligible because free from over-elaboration, of the ideas which govern the process of sorting from beginning to end, and shall indicate some changes of method which I would adopt had I to do the work over again.

4. The form of statistics required may vary from year to year. But whatever be the form that each separate table may take, it is advisable to consider carefully before commencing work how far these tables are interdependent, and how far the sorting accomplished for one table can be utilized towards diminishing the work involved in sorting for another.

5. Furthermore, it should be remembered that the figures appearing in any one table represent the sum of the totals arrived at by several clerks. It is an obvious advantage to diminish the number of these totals so far as possible; or in other words to give a large number of slips to each clerk. But the number of slips to be given to each clerk must be governed by the size of the unit for which statistical results are required. In Madras, "village statistics" showing the population of each village and each taluk by sex and religion, are published: it follows then that Imperial table VI, which shows the population of each district by religion and sex, and which represents the general result of the whole undertaking, must be built up from such particulars ascertained for every village in each district.

6. A glance will show that from this one sorting, which is facilitated by the fact that posted, but unsorted, slips have been tied up by villages, Imperial tables I to VI can be compiled. It is therefore above all things necessary to get the totals of religion and sex correct at this stage, for with these totals the sum of the details of all subsequent tables must agree. Theoretically such accuracy should be obtained by the vigilance of the checkers and supervisors, but to these, alas, the question "*quis custodiet ipsos custodes,*" frequently possesses a special relevance. A few precautions may be suggested in detail.

7. Slips, as already stated, have been bundled up by villages, and, even within these bundles, blocks have been tied up separately, with a label on the top of each block packet stating how many slips are contained therein. This label may be taken away, and the total number of slips in the packet counted by the sorter, whose counting abilities may thus be tested rapidly by the recorded results of the poster.

8. Again when the division by sex and religion has been made, the result may be checked, as to sex, by the provisional total recorded on the enumerators' abstracts, as to religion, by the exercise of a little commonsense. For example, a large number of Muhammadans at Srírangam or of Brahmos or Aryas in upland villages, can hardly fail to awaken some suspicion.

9. The distinction of religion and sex is always cropping up. So when religions and sexes have been separated let them remain apart.

10. Certain statistics are required separately for "cities" as well as for the districts in which they are included. The list of cities has been determined beforehand; therefore the slips for these cities may be preserved as separate units to the end.

11. Further particulars are required only by districts. But a district containing anything from one to three million inhabitants is an unwieldy sized thing to handle. Accordingly, while retaining the distinction of sex and religion, slips may be thrown together by taluks, and work henceforth carried out with the taluk as a unit.

12. We now proceed to table VII (age, sex, and civil condition). The sex distinction has already been established. The attempt was made at the present census to establish distinction as to civil condition during the first sorting for religion and sex. Inasmuch as the blank slips for posting had been arranged in the sorters' racks by religion, sex, and civil condition (*vide* Chapter II, paragraph 10), it was believed that the sorters would find little difficulty in putting back the slips in the pigeon-holes from which they had taken them out. The attempt was not successful, and was abandoned. Accordingly the slips of each religion must first be sorted by civil condition, and then according to the 19 prescribed age-periods.

13. Now in almost every taluk of the Presidency Hindus largely outnumber the sum total of every other religious community. It will therefore be expedient to divide Hindu slips between a certain number of clerks, and to assign all others to one or two men, thus allotting to each clerk in the section an approximately equal number of slips. Of course when "others" amount to but an insignificant total, these may be handed over to *one* of the clerks engaged with Hindus; his Hindu task being reduced proportionately.

14. Each clerk will then keep on sorting the same block of slips, (say 20,000—30,000), to the end of the chapter. It may be objected that, once he knows the total number allotted to him, he can always arrive at this total by the exercise of his imagination as to details. This can be avoided. The total of each religion and sex in every village has been ascertained by the first sorting; a supervisor giving out the slips for several villages to a clerk knows the total number given: from this he can take a few at random before sorting for any table commences, when the sorting ends, the clerk's total must fall short of the correct total by exactly the number of slips retained.

15. Two mistakes were made in 1911. The total number of slips given to each clerk was too small, and the clerk was required to count and add up the number of slips sorted for each table each day. The reasons for this second procedure, (which indirectly involved the first), were, first, the difficulty of ascertaining the number of sorted slips that would represent a fair day's work; secondly, the fact that many of the sorting offices were but long open sheds, in which it was undesirable to leave overnight large bundles of unsorted and uncounted slips. The rate of payment, after sundry alarms and excursions which included a mutiny, was fixed at As. 8 per 4,000 slips for all tables except XV (occupation), and for occasional special sortings; this rate I recommend to my successor. The highest average reached by any office on any one day was 12,019 (ordinary sorting), and 7,634 (occupation sorting). The result was the production of an infinite number of small totals, of which the compilation caused a vast amount of unncessary trouble.

16. After table VII, table VIII may be taken up. Before passing on to this, I may observe that the general division of age, sex, and civil condition in VII would seem to promise some help for XIV (age, sex, and civil condition, by selected castes). This hope, so far as I am aware, is unrealizable. In sorting for table VIII each religion and sex is divided into three groups, viz., (*a*) literate but not literate in English, (*b*) literate in English, (*c*) illiterate. The sum of (*a*) and (*b*) gives the total number of literates.

17. Literates, still more so literates in English, are unfortunately (or fortunately) rare in India. If a sorter is to be paid by results, it is scarcely fair to

measure his exertions by the few literary fish that he drags from the mighty ocean of illiteracy: on the other hand, if he stops to count his illiterate pile, he wastes a good deal of valuable time to no purpose. The difficulty may be solved thus: Keeping distinct his heaps, (*a*), (*b*) and (*c*), the sorter prepares X (parent tongue), and XI (birth-place), for each heap. The sum total of the three results gives him X and XI for all his slips; and at the same time the total of X or XI for heap (*c*) gives the number of uncounted illiterates for VIII. For this number he may take credit in VIII at the discretion of the Superintendent. The credit was allowed in 1911.

18. Still keeping separate these three heaps, (literate, literate in English, and illiterate), the sorter proceeds to do XIII (caste). The sorting, it is clear, gives automatically IX (education by selected castes).

19. Castes having been distinguished the selected castes may be sorted for table XIV.

20. I may here suggest the following procedure, which tends to prevent the multiplication of small totals in connection with tables VIII, X, XI, XIII, and XIV.

Sorting for table VIII has divided the population into literates and illiterates. Each man may sort his own illiterates for tables X and XI, but the literates of all sorters may be combined and sorted for these tables by one sorter. Similarly when XIII has been completed, the slips of castes selected for XIV may be collected together and sorted by one or two men for XIV.

21. Table XIII is a dreadful thing to prepare for a large city like Madras, and even for a district it is quite sufficiently troublesome. It is true that a reference to District Gazetteers will show that in every district there are certain main castes or tribes, which account for the majority of the population: labour is lightened by sorting for these castes and tribes primarily, and throwing everything else under the head "others." But the subsequent detailed sorting of these "others" is a sorrowful business. It has been suggested by one Deputy Superintendent that, as the taluk is the unit, each Tahsildar should be invited to furnish a list of the chief castes and tribes of his taluk. Unfortunately it is by no means certain that a Tahsildar would possess information on this point other than that which he found in the District Gazetteer.

22. Table XV (occupation) is generally accounted equal in the point of labour involved in its preparation to the sum total of all other tables. Inasmuch as a different system of classification of occupations is introduced at each decade, it is scarcely worth while to devote much space to the particular processes which produced the table in 1911. The detailed rules which guided the operation in that year will be found at pages 40 *et seq.* of the volume of Posting and Sorting Rules. A few suggestions may be made which will hold good for the preparing of any occupation table whatever may be its form.

23. This table should be prepared last of all, so that clerks may profit by experience gained in preparing previous tables. The number of clerks in each section should be reduced considerably by the exclusion of the unfit—a process which itself improves supervision.

24. Castes have been separated for table XIII. It is well to start occupation sorting with the slips still in their caste bundles, inasmuch as members of the same caste frequently follow the same occupation.

25. The results of the various processes of occupation sorting were noted down in certain "tickets" numbered I to VII which will be found at pages 30-36 of the volume of Abstraction and Compilation forms. A reference to these will facilitate comprehension of what follows.

26. Occupations in India fall under the two main heads of "agricultural" and "non-agricultural." Agriculturists form the majority of the population, and, among the non-agriculturists, there are usually certain predominant classes, such as "labourers unspecified," "general condiment dealers," etc.

27. In addition to the distinction of "principal occupations," it is generally necessary to discover (*a*) the subsidiary occupations followed by agriculturists; (*b*) the number of persons principally supported by a non-agricultural occupation, who follow agriculture as a subsidiary occupation.

28. Now a glance at the "occupation tickets" already referred to will show that ticket I embodied, generally speaking, particulars for the agricultural population, ticket IV for the non-agriculturists. But in ticket I were included in 1911 certain predominant non-agricultural occupations, the idea being to exhaust as many slips as possible in the first sorting. Entries made in ticket I for certain of these classes had subsequently to be transferred to the total of ticket IV.

29. Whatever be the modifications in detail introduced in 1921 it is fairly certain that the line of enquiry referred to in paragraph 26 will persist.

30. In 1921 I would utilize ticket I for agricultural occupations *only*, and transfer *all* non-agricultural occupations to ticket IV. If a "traditional occupation" is to be ascribed to certain castes, and statistics evolved on the basis of this idea, I would introduce another ticket in the following form:—

Caste and name of traditional occupation.	Number following traditional occupation without subsidiary occupation.	With agricultural subsidiary ation as occupation.	With other subsidiary occupation.	Following traditional occupation as subsidiary occupation.	Dependents.
1	2	3	4	5	6

Slips classified under columns 4 and 5 may be further sorted as required. Ticket IV, I would alter as follows:—

Occupation.	Group number.	Without subsidiary occupation.	With agricultural subsidiary occupation.	With other subsidiary occupation.	Dependents.	Total.
1	2	3	4	5	6	7

The sorting necessary to fill up this form should dispose completely of all non-agricultural occupations.

31. Further detailed sortings must be governed by a consideration of the results desired.

32. It is perhaps needless to observe that it is impossible to sort *directly* into any large number of heads. Non-agricultural occupations must be sorted first into not more than thirty general heads, (the sorting rack contains only thirty pigeon-holes), and slips found under each of these thirty heads sorted in greater detail. The thirty general heads used in 1911 will be found at page 45 of the volume of Posting and Sorting Rules; but these heads may be, (and generally were), varied at the discretion of the Deputy Superintendent of the office. This method of sorting is especially applicable to a city, where agricultural occupations account for very few of the inhabitants. The general heads used for the commencement of Madras city sorting were as follows :—

I. Police.
II. Railway.
III. Local and municipal.
IV. Post and telegraph.
V. Government service.
VI. Shopkeeper unspecified.
VII. Grain dealers.
VIII. Agriculture.
IX. Money-lender, pension, hotel, income allowance.
X. Army.
XI. Other specific shops.
XII. Betel, vegetable, nut, tobacco and snuff.
XIII. Milk dealer, baker and sweet-meat.
XIV. Butcher, fish and fruit.
XV. Grocer.
XVI. Cotton workers.
XVII. Book binders.
XVIII. Printers.
XIX. Tram and bandy.
XX. Cooly.
XXI. Mechanic.
XXII. Indoor servants.
XXIII. Brick and stone workers.
XXIV. Wood workers and painters.
XXV. Metal workers.
XXVI. Private clerks.
XXVII. Mendicants.
XXVIII. Religion and education.
XXIX. Doctor.
XXX. Lawyer.

33. *Compilation.*—Compilation is merely the adding up of the sorters' totals, and the copying them down in the forms prescribed for the Imperial and Provincial tables. If the sorters do their work accurately, and do not falsify totals, whether to swell their outturn or to save themselves trouble, this part of the work would hardly need mention.

34. Unfortunately the sorter, even with all the good-will in the world, is frequently inaccurate; and his inaccuracies frequently escape the notice of checkers and supervisors. Thus we find one figure representing the men of a district; another, the total of men single, married, and widowed; and yet a third, the total of men literate and illiterate in the same district.

35. It is well to commence compilation almost contemporaneously with sorting; and thus advance by a series of small but carefully tested totals. If compilation be postponed until sorting has concluded, mistakes will appear in the final totals; but it is then well nigh impossible to discover at what point such mistakes originated.

36. I obtained sanction for the employment of a special compilation office consisting of ten supervisors and fifty clerks (*vide* G.O. No. 692, Revenue, dated 13th March 1911); but I did not actually start with the office at this strength.

The plan did not work badly on the whole, but I found that a weak point was the absence of proper supervision. A man of at least the standing of a Deputy Superintendent is required for the control of this office.

The sorters' mutiny, referred to in paragraph 15 of this chapter, necessitated the removal of about 120 men from one of the sorting offices. The remaining sections of this office I distributed among other offices, and placed the Deputy Superintendent in charge of compilation. When sorting actually finished in some offices, I employed the Deputy Superintendents of such offices, with their best assistants, to clear off any arrears of compilation pending in the general compilation office.

37. I should recommend that in 1921, when posting is finished, a certain number of the posters of one office be distributed among the other offices, and the Deputy Superintendent thus relieved be placed in charge of compilation. His staff can be selected from the best men throughout all the offices. It must be remembered that in the six central offices two vernaculars, Tamil and Telugu, are employed, and accordingly the compilation staff must be formed in equal proportions of men who read and write each of these languages. It is an undoubted advantage if the Deputy Superintendent in charge of compilation is acquainted with both Tamil and Telugu.

38. These remarks apply only to the main offices dealing with Tamil and Telugu schedules. The comparatively small offices, which deal with Malayálam, Canarese and Oriyá, can, as a rule, manage their own compilation. They deal with small total populations, and mistakes can be detected, and rectified, without great difficulty.

CHAPTER IV.—FINANCE.

THE statements appended to this chapter show the total cost of the census. The work was done with every possible regard to economy, and, in respect of detail, I have no remarks to offer. I venture to leave on record one general opinion.

2. The slip system was new in 1901 ; accordingly the Superintendent of that year, (Mr. W. Francis), had to originate the excellent code of rules which we now follow. Ten years later, the increase in the cost of living necessitated more liberal payment of piece-workers ; that the cost of the 1911 census has not greatly exceeded that of its predecessor, is due to the fact that methods of work had been fixed by Mr. Francis, and thus little or no time was wasted on experiment. The piece workers, whose earnings form the chief item of expenditure, will probably be unable to work faster or better in 1921 than in 1911 ; but the cost of the necessaries to life will probably have increased considerably. It will therefore be necessary to offer more liberal terms to posters and sorters ; and accordingly, so far as I can foresee, the Superintendent of 1921 will have to resign himself to a considerably enhanced expenditure.

APPENDIX.

I.—Actual expenditure distributed under the heads of account prescribed by the Comptroller-General.

Main head.	Sub-head.	1910-11.	1911-12	1912-13.	Total.
1	2	3	4	5	6
	PERSONAL CHARGES.	RS.	RS.	RS.	RS.
Superintendence ...	Deputation allowance of officers deputed to census duty.	3,168	3,456	864	7,488
	ESTABLISHMENT.				
	Pay of men without substantive appointment, including famine batta.	517	600	116	1,233
	Deputation allowance of men deputed to census duty.	967	1,268	157	2,392
	Delhi coronation bonus	..	17	...	17
	TRAVELLING ALLOWANCE.				
	(i) Of officers	1,721	1,424	234	3,379
	(ii) Of establishment	465	96	32	593
	CONTINGENCIES.				
	Office rent	...	160	...	160
	Purchase and repair of furniture	4	...	...	4
	Local purchase of stationery	...	...	...	...
	Postage and telegram charges	403	90	58	551
	Freight	...	4	11	15
	Miscellaneous	75	314	137	526
Enumeration ...	Temporary establishment in district offices ...	...	2,205	...	2,205
	Remuneration of census officers	569	2,031		2,600
	Travelling allowance of census officers ...	46	3,927	1,535	5,508
	CONTINGENCIES.				
	Local purchase of stationery	2	83	...	85
	Postage	25	13	...	38
	House numbering	35	1,108	...	1,143
	Freight	826	404	...	1,230
	Miscellaneous	93	549	...	642
	ESTABLISHMENT.				
Abstraction and Compilation.	Pay of men without substantive appointment, including famine batta.	...	1,09,172	117	1,09,289
	Deputation allowance of officers deputed to census duty.	22	19,996	104	20.122
	Delhi coronation bonus	...	74	...	74
	Travelling allowance	70	1,073	...	1,143

I.—Actual expenditure distributed under the heads of account prescribed by the Comptroller-General—concluded.

Main head.	Sub-head.	1910-11.	1911-12.	1912-13.	Total.
1	2	3	4	5	6
	CONTINGENCIES.	RS.	RS.	RS.	RS.
Abstraction and Compilation—*cont.*	Office rent	..	1,943	...	1,943
	Petty construction and repairs	2,263	—381	...	1,882
	Purchase and repair of furniture	1,802	2,256	—125	3,933
	Local purchase of stationery	...	...	...	..
	Postage and telegram charges	...	518	.	518
	Freight	4	1,806	...	1,810
	Miscellaneous	34	1,528		1,562
Printing and other Stationery Charges.	Cost of stationery including paper supplied from central stores.	16,120	1,893	—323	17,690
	Carriage of stationery	1,753	...	...	1,753
	Printing—				
	(i) At Government presses	6,296	1,981	870	9,147
	(ii) At Private presses	3,931	1,766	...	5,697
	DESPATCHING CHARGES.				
	(i) Postage	...	...	...	...
	(ii) Other charges	95	—19	3	79
	ACTING ALLOWANCE OF OFFICERS IN NON-CENSUS OFFICES.				
Miscellaneous	(i) Officers	...	...	...	...
	(ii) Establishment—Pay including famine batta.	1,124	17,438	253	18,815
	TOTAL ...	42,430	1,78,793	4,043	2,25,266

II.—Expenditure distributed under the heads prescribed by the Census Commissioner, according to (a) *Comptroller-General's and* (b) *Departmental Accounts.*

Main head.	Sub-head.	Expenditure according to Comptroller-General's accounts. 1910-11.	1911-12.	1912-13.	Total, 1910-13.	Expenditure in 1910-13 according to departmental accounts.	Difference.	Remarks.
1	2	3	4	5	6	7	8	9
	I.—DISTRICT CHARGES.	RS.	RS.	RS.	RS.	RS.		
A.—Enumeration.	1. District office establishment.	...	2,205	..	2,205	2,205	...	...
	2. Remuneration of census officers.	569	2,031	...	2,600	2,600	...	...
	3. Travelling allowance of census officers.	46	3,927	1,535	5,508	5,508	...	...
	4. Contingencies—							
	(a) Petty stationery ...	2	83	...	85	85	...	...
	(b) Postage (for transmission of forms).	25	13	...	38	38	...	...
	(c) House numbering ...	35	1,108	...	1,143	1,143	..	...
	(d) Freight ...	826	404	...	1,230	1,230	..	...
	(e) Miscellaneous ...	93	549	...	642	642	..	...
	TOTAL I ...	1,596	10,320	1,535	13,451	13,451	...	...
	II.—PRESS CHARGES.							
	5. Paper	3,740		...	3,740	3,740	...	...
	6. Carriage of paper	972		...	972	972	...	...
	7. Printing—							
	(a) At Government presses.	5,502		...	5,502	5,502	...	...
	(b) At other presses ..	3,931	1,766	...	5,697	5,697	...	...
	8. Despatching charges ...	95	—19	3	79	79	...	...
	TOTAL II ...	19,240	1,747	3	20,990	20,990	...	...
	TOTAL, I and II ...	20,836	12,067	1,538	34,441	34,441	...	...

II.—Expenditure distributed under the heads prescribed by the Census Commissioner, according to (a) *Comptroller-General's and* (b) *Departmental Accounts*—continued.

Main head.	Sub-head.	Expenditure according to Comptroller-General's accounts. 1910-11.	1911-12.	1912-13.	Total, 1910-13.	Expenditure in 1910-13 according to departmental accounts.	Difference.	Remarks.
1	2	3	4	5	6	7	8	9
	III.—OFFICE CHARGES.	RS.	RS.	RS.	RS.	RS.		
B.—Tabulation of the Results.	9. Correspondence and accounts establishment—							
	(a) Pay of Government servants deputed to census duty.	24	941	94	1,059	1,086	+ 27	...
	(b) Deputation allowance of men deputed to census duty.	22	831	104	957	957	...	...
	(c) Pay of men without substantive appointment.		839	60	899	899	...	...
	10. Menial establishment—							
	Officials.							
	(a) Pay	...	47	...	47	47	..	...
	(b) Deputation allowance.	...	10	...	10	10	...	...
	Non-Officials.							
	(c) Pay of men without appointment.	...	5,996	57	6,053	6,053	...	...
	11. Working staff including superintendence—							
	Officials.							
	(a) Pay	...	14,930	...	14,930	21,596	+ 6,666	...
	(b) Deputation allowance.	...	19,155	...	19,155	19,155	...	...
	Non-Officials.							
	(c) Pay of men without substantive appointment.	...	1,02,337	...	1,02,337	1,02,337	...	...
	Delhi coronation bonus.	...	74	...	74	74	...	...
	12. Travelling allowance ...	70	1,073	...	1,143	1,143	...	...
	13. Contingencies—							
	(a) Rent	...	1,943	...	1,943	1,943	...	...
	(b) Furniture	1,802	2,256	— 125	3,933	3,933	...	...
	(c) Stationery	...	...	...	...	...	...	...
	(d) Postage	...	428	...	428	428	...	...
	(e) Telegrams	...	90	...	90	90	...	...
	(f) Freight	4	1,806	...	1,810	1,810	...	...
	(g) Miscellaneous .	34	1,528	...	1,562	1,562	...	...
	(h) Petty construction works.	2,263	— 381	...	1,882	1,882	...	...
	TOTAL III ...	4,219	1,53,903	190	1,58,312	1,65,066	+ 6,693	.
	IV.—PRESS CHARGES.							
	14. Paper for slips	6,805	...	...	6,805	6,805	...	...
	15. Paper for compilation ...	575	1,893	— 323	2,145	2,145	...	...
	16. Carriage of paper	781	...	...	781	781	...	...
	17. Printing—							
	(a) At Government presses.	794	...	...	794	794	...	...
	(b) At private presses ...	...	...	..	...	...	...	...
	18. Despatching charges ...	...	...	...	...	...	...	...
	TOTAL IV ...	8,955	1,893	— 323	10,525	10,525	...	...
	TOTAL B ...	13,174	1,55,796	— 133	1,68,837	1,75,530	+ 6,693	...

II.—Expenditure distributed under the heads prescribed by the Census Commissioner, according to (a) *Comptroller-General's and* (b) *Departmental Accounts*—concluded.

Main head.	Sub-head.	Expenditure according to Comptroller-General's accounts. 1910-11.	1911-12.	1912-13.	Total, 1910-13.	Expenditure in 1910-13 according to departmental accounts.	Difference.	Remarks.
1	2	3	4	5	6	7	8	9
	V.—PERSONAL CHARGES.	RS.	RS.	RS.	RS.	RS.		
C. Superintendence.	19. Pay of Superintendent ...	...		...	..	26,592	+ 26,592	...
	Exchange compensation allowance.	...	...	...	...	1,661	+ 1,661	...
	20. Deputation allowance of Superintendent.	3,168	3,456	864	7,488	7,800	+ 312	...
	21. Travelling allowance of Superintendent.	1,721	1,424	234	3,379	3,379	...	...
	TOTAL V ...	4,889	4,880	1,098	10,867	39,432	+ 28,565	...
	VI.—ESTABLISHMENT AND OFFICE CHARGES.							
	22. Superintendent's office establishment—							
	(a) Pay of Government servants deputed to census duty.	1,100	1,520	159	2,779	3,118	+ 339	...
	(b) Deputation allowance of men deputed to census duty.	967	1,268	157	2,392	2,392	...	...
	(c) Pay of men without appointment including famine batta.	517	600	116	1,233	1,233	...	...
	23. Travelling allowance of establishment.	465	96	32	593	593	...	...
	Delhi coronation bonus ...	...	17	...	17	17	...	..
	24. Printing—							
	(a) At Government presses.	...	1,981	870	2,851	2,851	...	...
	(b) At private presses ...	..	...	..	...	...	...	...
	25. Contingencies—							
	(a) Rent	...	160	...	160	160	...	...
	(b) Furniture ...	4	...	...	4	4	...	...
	(c) Stationery ...	...	...	...	...		...	...
	(d) Postage	357	85	56	498	498	...	...
	(e) Telegrams ..	46	5	2	53	53	...	...
	(f) Freight	...	4	11	15	15	...	...
	(g) Miscellaneous ...	75	314	137	526	526	...	...
	TOTAL VI ...	3,531	6,050	1,540	11,121	11,460	+ 339	...
	TOTAL C ...	8,420	10,930	2,638	21,988	50,892	+ 28,904	...
	GRAND TOTAL A, B, & C ..	42,480	1,78,993	4,048	2,25,266	2,60,863	+ 35,597	...

Note.—Rs. 14,373 have been taken in abatement of charges under the following heads:—

(a) Abstraction and Compilation.

		RS.
Pay of men without substantive appointment—		
Recoveries from District Municipalities ...		8,717
Do.	Coorg Municipalities ...	42
Do.	Pudukkóttai State	1,779
Do.	Banganapalle State ...	170
Do.	Sandur State ...	57
Do.	Madras Corporation ...	1,117
Contingencies—		
Sale-proceeds of furniture ...		1,221
Unspent amount from the advance for the repair of Gun Carriage Factory ...		381
Printing and other stationery charges, cost of stationery—Sale-proceeds of waste paper ...		356
(b) *Printing at Government Presses*—		
Cost of forms supplied to Cochin State ...		368
	Pudukkóttai ...	109
	Madras Corporation ...	56
	Total ...	14,373

Statement No. III appended to Chapter I does not include travelling allowance, etc., since sanctioned by Government to Ganjam, etc., districts. The Government contribution paid to the Madras Corporation (Rs. 5,031) has been included in the respective heads of account under enumeration.

THE CITY OF MADRAS

STATISTICAL TABLES

COMPILED ON THE OCCASION OF THE CENSUS OF 1911, WITH INTRODUCTORY NOTES

BY

J. CHARTRES MOLONY, I.C.S.,
Superintendent of Census, Madras,

AND

A CHAPTER ON THE INDUSTRIES OF THE CITY

BY

ALFRED CHATTERTON.

MADRAS:
PRINTED BY THE SUPERINTENDENT, GOVERNMENT PRESS.

[PRICE, 1 *rupee 2 annas.*] 1912. [1 *shilling 9 pence.*]

MADRAS AND ITS ENVIRONS

Scale 1 Inch = 1 Mile

Furlongs 8 6 4 2 0 1 2 Miles

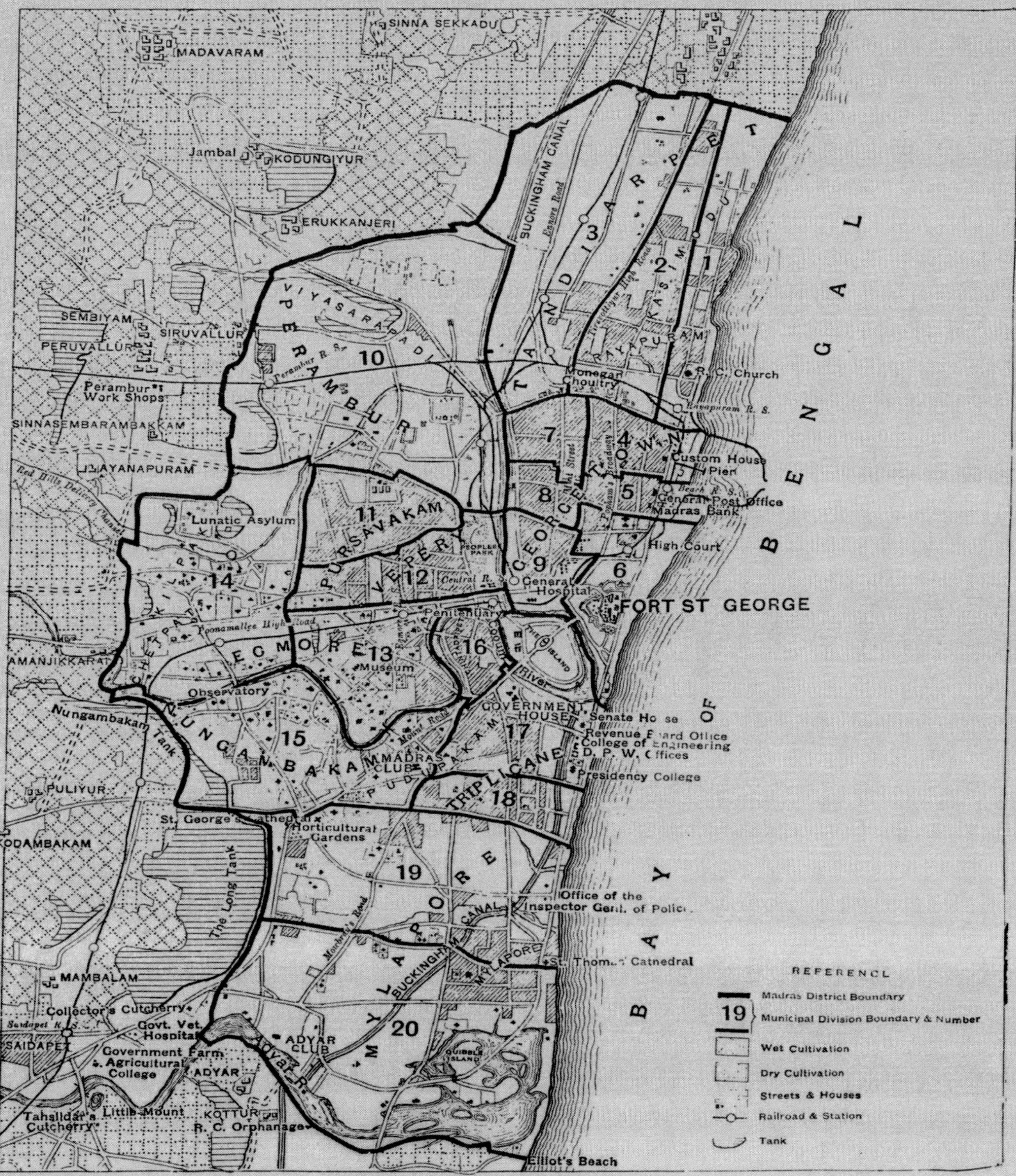

Reg No. 1964
Copies 400

Photo-Litho Survey Office, Madras.
1911

THE CITY OF MADRAS

STATISTICAL TABLES

COMPILED ON THE OCCASION OF THE CENSUS OF 1911, WITH INTRODUCTORY NOTES

BY

J. CHARTRES MOLONY, I.C.S.,

Superintendent of Census, Madras.

AND

A CHAPTER ON THE INDUSTRIES OF THE CITY

BY

ALFRED CHATTERTON.

MADRAS:

PRINTED BY THE SUPERINTENDENT, GOVERNMENT PRESS.

1912.

PREFACE.

In the reports written on the decennial enumerations of the Presidency, it has been of late the custom to treat Madras as a "district," and to devote a space necessarily brief to criticism of its advancement or decline as a whole. The liberality of the Madras Corporation has enabled me to publish the present statistics, which endeavour to exhibit the city, and its twenty municipal, divisions in the relation wherein the Imperial Report considers the Presidency and its districts.

No one can be more sensible than myself of the sins of omission and commission that may be cast up to this little volume. There is much in the tables that I would omit, and much wanting that I would add, were I to commence the work afresh; while I am sadly conscious of the baldness of my introductory remarks, when compared with the masterly report which Mr. Gover commenced forty years ago, but by the accident of death left unfinished. But if the publication is repeated, as I hope it will be, ten years hence, these imperfect tables will be at least material, which my successor may mould afresh and better; while my brief comments and criticisms may serve the purpose of pegs on which informing discussions may be hung.

My thanks are due to many for their aid in this work such as it is. To Mr. Alfred Chatterton for the chapter on industries which concludes the introduction; to Mr. J. W. Madeley and Dr. T. M. Nair for many helpful suggestions; to Messrs. T. Raghaviah and E. Nicholas for the care and accuracy with which they carried out the enumeration of the city. While here too, as in the more general work of the Presidency census, I have incurred large debts of energy and good-will to Messrs. S. Dandapani Aiyar and A. K. Kuppusami Aiyar of my personal office, and to Mr. T. Fisher, Superintendent of the Government Press.

Census Office, Vepery,
Madras,
1st *December* 1911.

J. CHARTRES MOLONY.

CONTENTS.

APPENDICES.

STATISTICAL TABLES

FOR THE

CITY OF MADRAS.

INTRODUCTORY REMARKS.

CHAPTER I.

MOVEMENT OF THE POPULATION IN THE CITY AS A WHOLE (TABLES I, II AND VI).

The movement of population in the city of Madras for the past forty years can be seen thus :—

1871	397,552
1881	405,848
1891	452,518
1901	509,346
1911	518,660

The decennial increase has been—

	Absolute.	Per cent.
1871–81	8,296	2·1
1881–91	46,670	11·5
1891–01	56,828	12·6
1901–11	9,314	1·8

Thus the increase, absolute and proportional, for the past decade is immeasurably below that of the preceding two decades. Although the absolute increase is slightly greater than that of the decade 1871–81, in which occurred the great famine of 1877, the percentage increase is lower.

It cannot be denied that these results have to a large extent falsified expectations. Numerous explanations can be given; of which the first and most obvious takes the form of an attack on the accuracy of the returns. But I do not think that there are any reasonable grounds for doubting that the returns are as correct as it is humanly possible to make them. The census arrangements made by Messrs. Raghaviah and Nicholas were admirably complete, and in the course of a long inspection on the census night I satisfied myself as to the care and precision with which they were carried out. In one way, it is true, the excellence of these arrangements may have caused a slight falling off in the totals in comparison with those of 1901, as extreme care was taken to avoid double enumeration.

I think then that we must look for explanation in what I shall call "mechanical" or "natural" causes.

By "mechanical" causes I understand removal of large defined bodies of men from city limits, cessation of large industries, or completion of large temporary works, removal of people to suburbs outside the city area, emigration and immigration. By "natural" causes I understand a growing unhealthiness of the city, or a diminishing fecundity of the people. Discussion of this latter question may best be postponed to Chapter III, which treats primarily of the age periods of the people.

Examination of what I have called "mechanical" causes demands an intimate knowledge of the industrial life of the city which I do not possess. I may however quote a few instances which have been suggested to me.

I understand that in 1901 some troops were stationed in the neighbourhood of Perambúr. These, with their followers, had been removed before March 10th, 1911 (the census night). Saddlery and harness works in the same neighbourhood had similarly ceased to exist.

The Gun Carriage Factory in Poonamallee road, which at the census of 1901 was employing some thousands of hands, had been closed down by the census time of 1911.

The following statement shows a total increase of 6,013 in certain residential quarters outside the city municipal limits :—

Name of place.	Population according to the census of 1911.			Population according to the census of 1901.		
	Total.	Males.	Females.	Total.	Males.	Females.
Kódambákkam	1,521	778	743	2,559	1,322	1,237
Saidapet Union	15,646	7,966	7,680	14,254	7,253	7,001
St. Thomas' Mount	15,546	7,794	7,752	15,571	7,623	7,948
Pallávaram	7,059	3,555	3,504	6,416	3,331	3,085
Sembiam Union	21,325	11,000	10,325	17,567	8,876	8,691
Villivákkam	923	461	462	704	354	350
Konnúr	1,978	992	986	1,398	723	675
Tiruvallúr Union	9,576	4,662	4,914	9,092	4,476	4,616
Total ...	73,574	37,208	36,366	67,561	33,958	33,603

No doubt all these causes may have contributed to the detriment of increase in the city. Yet even if we suppose their value to have been 15,000 in the decade, and add such number to the actual ascertained increase, we only get a total increase of 24,314 (or 4·8 per cent.), which still contrasts very unfavourably with the figures of the two preceding decades.

The following return taken from table VI is interesting in regard to emigration and immigration. It shows for successive decades the numbers of those who were born in Madras and were enumerated there, and the numbers of immigrants from other districts :—

—	1891.			1901.			1911.		
	Total.	Males.	Females.	Total.	Males.	Females.	Total.	Males.	Females.
* Born in Madras ...	325,846 / 382,908	159,872 / 186,775	165,974 / 196,133	348,723 / 402,813	171,769 / 197,971	176,954 / 204,842	345,317 / 403,325	172,729 / 199,849	172,588 / 203,476
Immigrants	127,172	66,445	60,727	160,623	84,961	75,662	173,343	93,736	79,607

* Numerator = Number of persons born in Madras and enumerated there.
Denominator = Total number of persons born in Madras.

These figures seem to indicate that between 1891 and 1901 it was becoming increasingly worth a man's while, if he was born in Madras, to remain there, while for the decade 1901–1911 the conditions seem to have been reversed. Women born in the city seem to be leaving it in increasing numbers; possibly owing to the rate for sons-in-law ruling lower in the mufassal than in the city; possibly because for caste and other social reasons the daughters of immigrants are given away in marriage at their ancestral homes.

Immigration figures show that the city is losing its attractiveness. An increase of 12,720 immigrants between 1901 and 1911 compares poorly with one of 33,451 between 1891 and 1901.

Table VI, to which a passing reference has been made already shows the district of birth returned by each person enumerated in the city. The following statement reduces it to a more comprehensible form :—

Birth place.	1911.	1901.	1891.
Madras Presidency.			
East Coast, North ...	13,418	12,373	12,555
Deccan ...	3,119	2,631	2,512
Madras City ...	345,317	348,723	325,346
East Coast, Central ...	109,287	109,787	80,420
Do. South ...	21,019	16,190	13,335
West Coast ...	4,415	2,498	1,845
Feudatories ...	1,312	713	591
Total ...	497,887	492,915	436,604
Outside the Presidency.			
Mysore ...	5,341	4,531	4,096
Bombay ...	2,614	1,920	1,260
Hyderabad ...	2,318	1,886	1,965
Other Provinces, etc. ...	5,318	3,515	3,446
Foreign Possessions ...	2,189	2,022	2,340
Rest of Asia ...	582	381	450
United Kingdom ...	2,003	1,908	1,597
Rest of Europe ...	244	124	171
Other places ...	164	144	589
Total ...	20,773	16,431	15,914
Grand Total ...	518,660	509,346	452,518

The most noticeable feature here is the state of immigration from the central and southern divisions of the "East Coast districts." Immigration from the southern division has increased steadily, if slowly, since 1891; while immigration from the central division, after exceptional progress from 1891 to 1901, fails to show any advance in the last decade. A consideration of the following figures localises this change in an apparent return to their homes of immigrants from North and South Arcot; and suggests furthermore that we should look for some local condition, which in the decade 1891–1901 led to a somewhat remarkable migration to Madras from Chingleput, North Arcot and South Arcot, and which has apparently now lost its force in the two latter districts though not in the first :—

District.	1911.	1901.	1891.
Chingleput ...	69,576	67,673	53,046
North Arcot ...	24,404	26,085	18,085
Salem ...	3,314	1,998	1,234
Coimbatore ...	2,134	1,463	936
South Arcot ...	9,859	12,568	7,119
Total ...	109,287	109,787	80,420

It may very possibly be that the spread of groundnut cultivation, essentially the small man's crop, is keeping the people of South Arcot at home.

But it is very questionable whether this drying up of the stream of immigration to the city is any cause for lamentation. It may be a sign, and I think it is a sign, that industry is spreading surely if slowly throughout the Presidency, instead of being confined to its capital town; that the labourer is growing more assured of a decent life in his own homeland, and more distasteful of the huddled dreariness of the city slums.

Finally we may glance at the question of extra-Indian emigration. For Burma, where, I am informed by Dr. Nair, mills are run well nigh entirely by Madras labour, 1,260,000 persons left the Presidency in the decade 1901–1901. Of these some 325,000 sailed from the Port of Madras. Less than one million have returned in the same period, the net loss to the Presidency being over 270,000. It is but fair to assume that a certain proportion of these emigrants were inhabitants of the city, while many more from the outside districts, had they not gone to Burma, would have drifted into Madras.

CHAPTER II.

THE CITY DIVISIONS (TABLE II).

Table II shows the variation in population of each division since 1891.

It will be noticed that between 1891 and 1901 all divisions except I, V and VI showed an increase. In 1911 eight divisions show a falling off; but curiously enough division V has changed from decided decrease to decided increase. Of this however a very probable explanation has been suggested to me by Mr. J. W. Madeley. It is that at the census of 1901 the figures of divisions IV and V got mixed up, and a number of the inhabitants of V were credited to IV. Division IV in that year showed an increase of 5,839, which was somewhat strikingly great; while V showed a decrease of 2,852 when all adjacent divisions were increasing, or if losing, losing very slowly. Transfer (say) 3,000 from IV to V, and we have in 1901 an increase of 2,839 in IV, with one of 148 in V; a much more probable state of affairs. Then in 1911 we shall have a decrease of 292 in IV, with one of 1,378 in V.

In the period 1891 to 1911 all but four divisions (I, V, VI, IX) show an increase; and of these four, No. V, if the figures are to be accepted, has turned towards increase in the past ten years.

In the divisions increasing in 1901–1911 the rate of increase falls below that of the decade 1891–1901, except in the case of XX (Mylapore), where it has risen from 11·6 per cent. to 20·6; XIV (Kilpauk) 7·5 per cent. to 23·1; XII which remains constant. Here a reference to table IV may help consideration of the question whether there is in any division an increase in the vigorous section of the population, or whether there is a silting up of young children and old people.

A well nigh continuous decline in the proportion of females to males may be noticed. At the same time it must be admitted, that this phenomenon was almost as marked in the preceding decade of great increase as in the present one.

We may consider the separate city divisions with reference to their actual physical state.

By the side of the sea, division I has suffered to some extent from erosion. Some houses may have been lost, and nobody is likely to build on the ground overhanging the water's edge. But, on going a little inland, there seems to be no reason save one why the northern divisions should not improve, unless malaria is creeping in from Ennúr. They should not be inherently more unhealthy than such divisions as X, XI, XII, etc., granted the housing obtainable in both quarters to be equally good. Indeed it may be observed that the percentage of children in these divisions is high (Table IV), which suggests that the locality is "residential" and not unhealthy. But the obvious reason why people avoid the extreme north-east of the city is that communications are bad—there are no tramways. If the bread-winner's work is far away, he has no cheap and easy means of getting to it.

Divisions IV, V, VII and VIII are the very heart of the city. Their population is the "fighting line" of industry, whose vacancies are likely to be filled up by adult immigrants rather than by natural increase. This view is borne out by the age distribution table. It is doubtful whether population here *can* expand more. The sea front is now covered with large blocks of business premises, and the tendency of modern times is for such to expand. There is no room left for small residential houses, procurable at a price that suits the shallow pocket or exiguous dhoti end. And Madras, it may be noted, is essentially a one storied, or at most two storied city. The enterprise of its landlords, and the inclination of its inhabitants, show no signs of materialising in the sky-scaling rabbit warrens of Bombay. Furthermore, although the reflection is hardly relevant to a particular locality, it may be queried whether extension of large industries and commerce is so likely to account for an increase in population in Southern India as in western countries. The characteristic of industry in India is an abundant supply of cheap, and on the whole rather inefficient labour, which machinery and a smaller number of skilled workmen tend to supplant: the same observation applies to commerce, where one may notice a horde of low-paid clerks doing the work entrusted to one fairly well-paid man in Europe.

With VI, XVI, XVII we come to large open spaces, such as the Fort Glacis, the surroundings of the High Court, the Island, Government House and Park, Napier Park, etc. There is no likelihood of these being turned into residential quarters, and consequently no great increase need be expected.

Looking at X and XIV we can descry considerable possibilities of increase. The big mills in X absorb a good deal of space, but a great deal of the rest of Perambúr would bear a thicker settlement without inconvenience. Moreover the geographical position of Sembiam, Siruvallúr, and some few others, suggests the boon (doubtless an appreciated boon for the inhabitants) of inclusion in Madras municipal limits.

Purasawakkam (XI) is fairly thickly settled, so is XII (Vepery). When we pass to Kilpauk (XIV) we get the first inklings of a question applicable to all the remaining western and southern divisions of the city. There is plenty of vacant space, but this space is represented by the large private compounds that stand for the chief excellence and amenity of Madras. Are these to fall a prey to the jerry builder, and if they do, will this be for the good or ill of the city?

Some few remarks as to the general aspects of city life may serve as a conclusion to this chapter and to its predecessor.

Of primary importance to the growth of a city are (*a*) good work with good wages; (*b*) health; (*c*) amusement.

Wages are on the whole good in Madras; that is to say the profit of a higher rate of pay than obtains in the country is not entirely swept away by increase in the cost of living. There are indications of a coming demand for well-paid labour: such as the introduction of water-works and drainage throughout the city, the probable extension of the use of electricity (including tramway extension), the alteration of the old Gun Carriage Factory into a Public Works Department Workshop, the building of a new Government Press, etc.

As regards health, the "plain common Indian," it is true, does not study the disquisitions of health officers. His simple criterion of salubrity is whether a place is feverish or not feverish: infantile mortality, which subsequent consideration will perhaps show as the root cause of Madras' tardy increase, the man in the street is apt to look upon as the unaccountable whim of Heaven.

But that all is well with the health and sanitation of Madras, not even its most admiring city father will assert, when he considers its death-rate: very possibly the same idea is beginning to strike home to his simpler brother. He has but to consider the Cooum (for the betterment of which savoury stream a project is now on foot), or recall the remark of a touring politician, who, when asked to visit a sewage farm, replied innocently that he thought he was already on the spot.

The attractions of "amusement" are far less potent in the east than in the west. The glamour of the music hall, which attracts the European rustic from the deadly dullness of the country side, has not its counterpart here. It is as easy and meritorious to feed Brahmans in the country village as in the city; and the national hot weather pastime of litigation can be enjoyed as well, as profitably, and as securely, before the District Munsif as in the High Court of Judicature.

CHAPTER III.

THE AGES OF THE POPULATION (TABLES III AND IV).

In this chapter to a consideration of the question of age we may add that of sex and civil condition, and thus perchance arrive at some conclusions as to the "natural causes" of increase or decrease alluded to in chapter I.

The following statement shows the movement and position of the population at certain age periods with reference to the same three fixed points: the enumerations of 1891, 1901 and 1911 :—

HINDU.

Age period.	1891.	1901.	Variation.	1911.	Variation.
0-10	85,104	96,675	+ 11,571	91,774	− 4,901
10-20	64,338	80,013	+ 15,675	81,900	+ 1,887
20-40	124,757	138,240	+ 13,483	147,350	+ 9,110
40 and over	84,798	95,720	+ 10,922	94,886	− 834
Total ...	358,997	410,648	+ 51,651	415,910	+ 5,262

MUHAMMADAN.

Age period.	1891.	1901.	Variation.	1911.	Variation.
0-10	12,222	13,025	+ 803	13,016	− 9
10-20	9,841	11,661	+ 1,820	12,244	+ 583
20-40	16,975	18,340	+ 1,365	19,969	+ 1,629
40 and over	14,146	14,305	+ 159	13,940	− 365
Total ...	53,184	57,331	+ 4,147	59,169	+ 1,838

CHRISTIAN.

Age period.	1891.	1901.	Variation.	1911.	Variation.
0-10	9,901	9,906	+ 5	9,587	− 319
10-20	8,821	9,312	+ 491	9,136	− 176
20-40	12,808	13,171	+ 343	14,343	+ 1,192
40 and over	8,212	8,589	+ 377	8,746	+ 157
Total ...	39,742	40,958	+ 1,216	41,812	+ 854

The age periods that I have selected I take to represent childhood, adolescence, the prime of life, and its decline. We note that 1901, as compared with 1891, shows a decided increase at each period in each religion. Of these four periods, the most likely to be affected by unfavourable circumstances are the first and last, namely childhood and old age. Consequently it is not surprising to find that in a decade apparently unfavourable, the small increase that has occurred is entirely in the strong sections of adolescence and manhood, while the extreme periods have changed from a positive increase to positive decrease.

Confining our attention to the rising generation, who after all are of most importance to the growth of the city, we find that among Hindus (who represent four-fifths of the population), the 1891 children of the age period 0–10 were 85,104. At the next enumeration these are represented by those in the age period 10–20, who number 80,013, thus showing a loss of 5,091. Drawing a comparison between similar age periods in 1901 and 1911, we find that the wastage is well nigh trebled and stands at 14,775.

Now the question arises whether this apparent falling off in children is due to a lack of possible parents to produce children, or the inability of such parents to preserve their children alive when born.

It is, I think, a fair assumption that a male Madrasi is most likely to beget children between the ages of 20 and 45, and a female to produce them between the ages of 15 and 35. People at these times of life I shall term "reproductive," and of these there were and are as follows :—

Year.	Males.	Females.
1891	93,121	86,372
1901	104,739	94,099
1911	113,212	97,893

I may mention that in 1901 quinquennial age periods were not distinguished between 20 and 40, and 40, and 60. I have therefore had to obtain the necessary figures for 1901 by calculations based on the data of 1891.*

One point strikes us, namely the steadily growing disproportion between males and females. The total increase of 56,828 between 1891 and 1901 was made up of an increase of 30,913 in males, and 25,915 in females. In the decade 1901–1911, while males increased by 9,735, females decreased by 421. The deficiency of suitable mates for the men of 1891 was slightly under 7,000; this has grown to over 10,000 in 1901, and to well nigh 16,000 in 1911.

Now the children aged 0–10 at the enumeration of 1901 probably represent those that the reproductive people of 1891 were able to produce and keep alive. These numbered 119,596. Such children in 1911, attributable to the reproductive people of 1901, number 114,377. We have therefore a larger number of possible parents to account for a smaller number of children. I have disregarded the influences of immigration and emigration of children, and have also left out of account parents and children, (they are very few), outside the main religions, Hindu, Muhammadan and Christian.

This statement of persons at reproductive ages represents what we may call the raw material of matrimony. The following figures show the use made thereof. I trust that the crudeness of my expressions will not bring a blush to the modest cheek of my readers.

Statement showing persons married at reproductive ages.

Year.	Males.	Females.
1891	68,768	69,980
1901	74,896	73,442
1911	82,044	78,808

These figures are somewhat striking. We notice that in 1891 there were enough and to spare of reproductive women for the men actually married (an excess of 1,212); in 1901 this has changed to a deficiency of 1,454, and this deficiency has risen to 3,236 in 1911.

Comparing the two sets of figures, we find that there were at the present census 31,168 males at the reproductive period of life, who returned themselves as unfettered by domestic cares. Should they desire to change their state, there were apparently but 19,085 brides of suitable age: the reality is somewhat worse than the appearance, for included in this total were 7,272 Hindu widows, who, for the purposes of increase, are presumably useless to the community.

We may now look at the Sanitary Commissioner's vital statistics for the last two decades.

Decade.	Births.			Deaths.			Excess of deaths over births.
	Total.	Males.	Females.	Total.	Males.	Females.	
1891–1900	178,349	91,385	86,964	183,432	90,298	93,734	5,083
1901–1910	191,903	98,573	93,330	219,610	110,213	109,397	27,707

* A most unsatisfactory method. For it tacitly assumes that divergent tendencies produce identical results; or *vice versâ*.

The conclusion would seem to be that the difficulty lies, not so much in the producing of children, as in the keeping them alive when born. The fact that in the latter decade male deaths exceed female is of some significance. The general proportion may be assumed to extend to children; and though in earliest infancy male deaths in most countries exceed female, this general tendency may be assumed as neutralised in India by the undoubtedly greater solicitude shown for boys. Thus the preponderance of male deaths over female suggests that the causes of death have in the past decade been more numerous or more urgent than in the decade preceding.

We may now look at another question arising from a consideration of Table III. Even social reformers, most conservative of mankind, admit that there is little to be said for a system which burdens a boy with a wife, and the possibility of a family, before he is at an age to support either; and exposes an undeveloped girl to the stresses of sexual intercourse and maternity.

Assuming that a male should not marry until he has passed his twentieth and a girl till she has passed her fifteenth year we have the following comparative statement of persons who are, but who ought not to be, married.

Year.	Hindus.		Muhammadans.		Christians.	
	Males.	Females.	Males.	Females.	Males.	Females.
1901	2,640	4,513	194	413	59	76
1911	2,653	4,456	222	385	30	52

Here, one is glad to notice, Madras shows a real advance, inasmuch as it has not, on the whole, gone backwards in a space of ten years.

CHAPTER IV.

EDUCATION (TABLE V).

On a general view the progress of education, (or at least literacy), in the city would appear to be satisfactory. The standard of literacy adopted at this census and at that of 1901 was ability to write a letter and to read the answer to it. A brief comparative statement is subjoined :—

Year.	Hindus.				Muhammadans.				Christians.			
	Literate.		Literate in English.		Literate.		Literate in English.		Literate.		Literate in English.	
	Males	Females.	Males.	Females.	Males.	Females.	Males.	Females	Males.	Females.	Males.	Females.
1901	70,399	12,179	24,947	534	9,457	1,049	2,202	17	12,310	9,828	8,853	7,079
1911	86,630	19,681	34,592	1,089	11,674	2,135	3,056	74	13,045	10,516	10,143	7,424

Progress may be seen more clearly if the percentages of literates to total population at the two enumerations are compared.

Year.	Hindus.		Muhammadans.		Christians.	
	Percentage of literates to population.		Percentage of literates to population.		Percentage of literates to population.	
	Male.	Female.	Male.	Female.	Male.	Female.
1901	33·8	6	31	3·6	60	48
1911	40·4	9	38	7	63	50

When looking at these proportional figures we must bear in mind the general movement of population in the decade, which has been as follows :—

	Male.	Female.
Hindus	+ 6,445	— 1,183
Muhammadans	+ 1,879	— 41
Christians	+ 517	+ 337

It is thus evident that the improvement in the percentage of literacy, especially among Hindu and Muhammadan women, is not due to any considerable diminution of the total numbers.

The great superiority of Christians in point of literacy is to be accounted for by the presence of a large number of Europeans and Eurasians in their ranks; and by the fact that education is a most prominent feature in the missionary's scheme of things. "Rice and schools," a missionary once wrote to me, "will convert any number of Paraiyans"; to me they seem most excellent reasons for a change in one's theology. The returns of female education appear especially noteworthy. Education, with all its defects in India, is the key to progress. Women form one half of every community; 91 per cent. of this Hindu half, and 93 per cent. of the Muhammadan half, still lack the key. The Christians with 50 per cent. of their women literate *must* forge ahead, whatever be the disadvantages with which they start. That Hindus and Muhammadans appear to recognise this fact will be evident from a few subsequent figures.

The vitality or progress of education may, generally speaking, be judged by the variation in the proportion of educated children to educated adults. If the proportion falls, then an uneducated generation is growing up : if it rises, then we may look for improvement among the coming adults, who are to be the strength of the community. The following figures show the proportion of literates aged 0–15 to 1,000 literates aged 20 and over.

Religion.	Males.		Females.	
	1901.	1911.	1901.	1911.
All religions	181	166	450	385
Hindu	175	162	496	423
Muhammadan	133	136	341	320
Christian	258	221	409	333

Now these figures look discouraging, but a little reflection shows that the bogie set up may very easily be knocked down. These figures are, I believe, the result of that falling off in the total number of children to which reference has already been made. This fact is indeed made abundantly clear by the following statement :—

Religion.	Proportional increase or decrease of population at age 0–15.		Proportional increase or decrease of literates at age 0–15.	
	Male.	Female.	Male.	Female.
	1901 to 1911.	1901 to 1911.	1901 to 1911.	1901 to 1911.
All religions	− 3·8	− 5·4	+ 12·8	+ 26·8
Hindu	− 4·9	− 6·4	+ 15·3	+ 46·0
Muhammadan	+ 2·8	− 1·6	+ 25·0	+ 95·9
Christian	− 4·3	− 3·5	− 6·0	− 7·1

Thus we see that while children have decreased in numbers, they have improved in education. For we cannot draw the improving but improbable conclusion that Heaven kills off the naughty children, who will not attend to their lessons. The figures in regard to Christian education are worth consideration, as they may tend to show that Christians are losing ground, while Hindus and Muhammadans are gaining. Especially is this the case with regard to female education, but the figures must be taken with some reservations. For when *absolute* numbers are very small, *proportional* figures are easily influenced, and are apt to be misleading.

Finally I append two statements showing proportional figures of literacy, and literacy in English, for each main religion at certain age periods in each division of the city. They may be of interest to future founders of schools.

Percentage of literates to population at certain ages by religions, sexes and divisions (1911).

Division.	0–15.						20 and over.					
	Males.			Females.			Males.			Females.		
	Hindu.	Musalman.	Christian.	Hindu.	Musalman.	Christian.	Hindu.	Musalman.	Christian.	Hindu.	Musalman.	Christian.
I ...	4·8	7·1	22·2	2·2	0·8	26·6	23·1	35·8	68·3	2·9	3·5	43·9
II ...	9·5	8·5	20·6	2·2	1·9	16·8	34·9	50·4	66·8	3·6	5·1	41·9
III ...	10·6	8·7	17·1	3·1	2·4	13·7	31·6	57·5	64·4	4·4	6·2	26·0
IV ...	19·9	12·8	36·7	12·5	5·6	33·3	57·8	51·5	86·7	11·4	9·0	80·0
V ...	25·4	25·0	31·5	13·2	10·3	45·3	64·4	69·2	85·3	13·5	12·8	66·6
VI ...	18·7	15·3	26·4	9·5	5·8	19·3	58·8	54·4	87·9	12·1	8·5	52·7
VII ...	24·6	4·4	35·1	14·0	1·7	30·7	69·6	36·1	87·4	19·4	4·0	65·4
VIII ...	20·8	16·2	33·3	11·3	...	20·0	65·0	74·4	47·8	16·6	2·7	42·9
IX ...	15·6	20·0	29·7	5·2	15·8	27·6	64·6	69·7	89·7	7·9	3·0	79·9
X ...	8·4	13·1	19·7	2·2	4·0	7·6	33·6	54·0	81·3	3·0	9·1	54·2
XI ...	15·3	4·1	31·4	6·4	8·4	29·0	49·6	54·4	81·1	7·5	8·5	66·9
XII ...	17·9	17·8	31·4	7·5	3·4	39·0	55·5	69·0	85·1	8·9	8·0	68·4
XIII ...	16·6	16·6	27·6	8·2	3·4	24·8	46·6	53·9	82·0	11·0	6·5	57·6
XIV ...	11·8	12·3	69·0	2·7	8·7	63·6	26·5	21·7	83·4	3·2	1·8	63·5
XV ...	11·7	10·7	26·8	4·4	6·9	24·9	44·7	50·1	88·5	5·7	8·9	53·2
XVI ...	17·3	11·0	28·0	7·4	5·9	25·5	58·7	61·7	80·9	10·1	11·7	53·4
XVII ...	16·9	14·0	15·3	8·1	4·7	29·0	59·7	45·5	87·4	10·0	8·6	69·2
XVIII ...	19·1	10·4	34·2	9·8	5·8	16·8	61·9	50·5	89·4	13·7	10·3	51·0
XIX ...	11·9	9·5	29·4	4·1	2·6	34·9	42·4	39·4	79·7	6·2	7·8	50·8
XX ...	16·8	11·5	26·6	7·5	6·7	23·9	45·9	44·1	70·8	10·2	8·1	44·4
Total ...	15·8	12·3	29·5	7·1	4·5	30·0	51·6	50·5	81·2	9·6	8·3	57·3

Percentage of literate in English at certain age periods to total literates at that age in Madras city, by divisions.

Division.	Males.				Females.			
	0–15.	15–20.	20 and over.	Total.	0–15.	15–20.	20 and over.	Total.
I	42·1	54·3	45·8	46·2	55·7	57·1	49·0	52·2
II	27·8	41·4	28·1	29·4	14·9	9·8	20·5	17·4
III	31·0	21·1	32·2	32·2	4·9	11·8	8·4	8·3
IV	31·9	56·5	44·0	44·7	13·4	11·3	16·1	14·5
V	48·2	64·5	52·5	53·4	38·3	34·8	40·4	38·8
VI	40·6	50·9	46·8	46·6	20·2	16·5	25·2	22·6
VII	36·4	61·4	53·8	52·4	11·3	13·1	13·8	13·1
VIII	26·8	46·5	37·4	37·4	4·7	4·6	2·5	3·3
IX	29·9	40·0	30·2	31·3	21·0	28·8	34·0	30·8
X	22·5	25·5	27·3	26·5	9·3	14·3	24·9	20·1
XI	33·3	44·8	38·2	38·3	23·7	30·2	37·4	32·9
XII	34·3	46·5	43·2	42·3	40·9	46·2	51·8	48·1
XIII	43·6	58·9	48·7	49·2	35·8	36·3	44·6	41·4
XIV	48·8	55·3	41·6	44·8	53·4	55·8	66·0	60·2
XV	20·1	52·7	46·7	44·0	15·7	29·9	46·4	36·4
XVI	42·0	50·3	45·0	45·3	20·6	24·8	29·2	26·3
XVII	34·6	61·0	44·6	45·6	9·6	9·5	12·1	11·0
XVIII	42·2	64·7	49·4	50·5	4·0	7·2	7·1	6·4
XIX	30·0	46·2	38·3	38·1	27·9	36·3	31·7	31·7
XX	41·0	59·5	45·1	46·3	27·0	29·9	32·8	30·8
Total ...	35·8	51·2	42·6	42·8	23·4	24·9	28·4	26·6

CHAPTER V.

CASTE, RACE AND RELIGION (TABLES VII AND VIII).

Table VII gives us the caste, tribe, race and religion returned by every person at the last enumeration.

Disquisitions on racial peculiarity or social custom are out of place in dealing with the progress of a modern city. I shall only make use of this table in so far as it may enable us to localise certain details in the movement of the population.

Dealing first with Hindus, we get the following figures :—

Caste according to linguistic division.	1901.				1911.			
	Males.	Females.	Total.	Surplus or defect of women.	Males.	Females.	Total.	Surplus or defect of women.
Tamil	149,364	147,996	297,360	− 1,368	149,852	143,313	293,165	− 6,539
Telugu	48,123	47,564	95,687	− 559	49,757	47,909	97,666	− 1,848
Malayálam	573	100	673	− 473	1,270	218	1,488	− 1,052
Canarese	1,229	949	2,178	− 280	1,967	1,504	3,471	− 463
Oriya	73	119	192	+ 46	86	24	110	− 62
Other Madras ...	7,260	6,151	13,411	− 1,109	10,309	8,903	19,212	− 1,406
Other Foreign ...	593	435	1,028	− 158	296	214	510	− 82
Not stated ...	71	48	119	− 23	194	94	288	− 100
Total ...	207,286	203,362	410,648	− 3,924	213,731	202,179	415,910	− 11,552

Now the first point that strikes us in these figures, is the fact that, while Hindus show an increase of 5,262, this figure is reached by a decrease of 4,195 in the Tamil castes, and an increase of 9,457 elsewhere. Furthermore the decrease in Tamil castes is entirely on the female side : men have increased by 488, while women have decreased by 4,683. The disproportion between the sexes of the Tamil castes, which in 1901 was 1,368, has now risen to 6,539 ; and this to a large extent accounts for a sex disparity of 11,552 in the Hindu population, and one of 11,270 in the total population of the city.

It is not on the whole surprising that this sex disparity should be found in castes other than Tamil ; such are immigrants to the city, and may be expected to leave their women folk behind them ; thus an increasing disparity may be accounted for by increasing immigration. But that this disparity should be in the increase among the Tamils in their own chief city is certainly curious.

We may endeavour to localise this divergence somewhat more closely—

Caste.	1901.			1911.		
	Males.	Females.	Disparity.	Males.	Females.	Disparity.
Bráhman	8,330	6,126	− 2,204	12,055	8,672	− 3,383
Kammálan	7,963	7,533	− 430	7,916	7,710	− 206
Palli	25,644	25,921	+ 277	26,069	24,140	− 1,929
Valluvan	752	726	− 26	2,035	893	− 1,142
Vannán	942	907	.. 35	2,660	1,550	− 1,110
Vániyan	10,480	9,992	− 488	7,416	8,080	+ 664
Total ...	54,111	51,205	− 2,906	58,151	51,045	− 7,106

We notice here a somewhat disproportionate increase of Bráhmans, which increase is most marked on the male side. It is possible to account for this by the well known fact that Kammálans have commenced to find a strange satisfaction in calling themselves Bráhmans. Their total number has remained practically stationary (which is improbable), while their sex ratio has completely changed. It may be possible that Kammálans male and female have changed themselves into Bráhmans, but that owing to the innate conservatism of females the change has been less marked among them.*

Pallis have actually decreased in total numbers while their sex ratio has changed. A plausible explanation would be the desire on the part of the Pallis to style themselves Kshatriyas; a desire shared by Shánáns. The following figures lend corroboration to this view :—

Caste.	1901.				1911.			
	Males.	Females.	Total.	Sex disparity.	Males.	Females.	Total.	Sex disparity.
Palli	25,644	25,921	51,565	+ 277	26,069	24,140	50,209	– 1,929
Shánán	4,944	4,958	9,902	+ 14	3,971	3,745	7,716	– 226
Kshatriya	611	544	1,155	– 67	4,291	4,175	8,466	– 116

These figures suggest that a considerable number of Tamils have transferred themselves to the Kshatriya ranks and so swelled the numbers of "Madras—other languages" castes, and that in this transference sex proportions have become mixed. The following figures repeated give a succinct view of the question :—

Madras Castes—"Other Languages."

1901.				1911.			
Males.	Females.	Total.	Sex disparity.	Males.	Females.	Total.	Sex disparity.
7,260	6,151	13,411	– 1,109	10,309	8,903	19,212	– 1,406

Vannáns and Vániyans it is obvious have become mixed either in 1901 or in 1911. Schedules for the city were filled up in English, and the facilities for confusion are obvious.

The figures for Valluvans are inexplicable, and though they appear to swell the Tamil castes, they exercise a disturbing influence on sex ratio. The only explanation that I can suggest is that females of the caste may have returned themselves as Paraiyans, although this conjecture is not supported by figures either as regards total increase or maintenance of sex ratio. In 1901 Paraiyan women exceeded the men by 950; in 1911 by 473 only.

As regards Muhammadans and Christians no question appears to arise.

Those classed as others (Jew, Buddhist, Parsi, etc.), show a decided increase from a total of 404 (male 272, female 132) in 1901, to 1,769 (male 1,168, female 601) in 1911. As a reason therefor we may assign the presence of some Buddhist missionaries in the city, and an increased immigration of Parsis. The sex ratio of the city has been influenced somewhat by these figures. There is in women a natural slowness to change an ancient faith (on the side of Buddhist conversion), and a natural tendency for immigrants to leave their women folk behind.

* Still in India a man generally gives the return for his women folk. If he returns himself as a Bráhman, he will hardly return his wife as a Kammálan.

CHAPTER VI.

INFIRMITY (TABLE IX).

Table IX shows the sufferers from leprosy, insanity, blindness and deaf-mutism throughout the city. I question whether any conclusion can be drawn from it. Taking leprosy first, the great predominance of lepers in Division II is due to the fact that the leper hospital is situated there. As regards the rest of the city I doubt whether the return is accurate. Leprosy, especially among females, is not generally the subject of advertisement.

Insanity is localised in Division XIV, where is the Lunatic Asylum. Again the completeness of the return may be doubted. A person must be very mad in India before lunacy will be admitted by his or her relatives; still more so before the patient is placed under restraint.

I give for what they are worth the comparative figures of 1901 and 1911. A decrease in blindness is noticeable; but a return of 175 blind people in a population of over half a million appears to be grotesquely inaccurate.

Infirmity.	1901.			1911.		
	Males.	Females.	Total.	Males.	Females.	Total.
Leprosy	299	94	393	200	72	272
Insanity	355	121	476	452	173	625
Blindness	158	123	281	87	88	175
Deaf-mutism	92	60	152	129	68	197

CHAPTER VII.

THE INDUSTRIES OF MADRAS (TABLE X).

(*By Alfred Chatterton.*)

Although Madras is in respect to population the third city in India, it is, from an industrial point of view, of small importance. Founded as a factory of the East India Company in the year 1640, it owes its growth to political rather than economic causes. Before the advent of railways and steamers it was as conveniently situated as any other town on the surf-bound Coromandel Coast for trading, and, as the centre of the East India Company's administration, it gradually grew into commercial importance, and ultimately, as the capital of the Southern Presidency, it became a city with a large population. In the middle of the nineteenth century it was relatively a town of greater industrial importance than it is now, as in those days indigenous industries flourished, and there were a number of important Government factories. When the East India Company ceased to carry on trade, the foreign business passed almost entirely into the hands of European houses of Agency, and although they displayed considerable enterprise in endeavouring to establish industries on a large scale in the country, their efforts met with little success, and up to the present day trade has proved more remunerative than manufacture. The reasons for this may be summarised briefly:—

(1) The natural poverty of the country and the lack of raw materials as a basis for manufacturing operations.

(2) The indigenous industries were of a very primitive type and entirely in the hands of uneducated artizans.

(3) The non-official European community was drawn more from the commercial than the manufacturing classes, and their natural inclination was rather to finance agriculture and develop trade, than risk their capital in industrial work, of which they had but little practical knowledge.

(4) The limited market for specialised manufactures, due to the poverty of the people and the want of facilities for transport.

In respect to fuel, a large and cheap supply of which is essential to the establishment of modern industries, Madras is severely handicapped. The nearest coal field is at Singareni in the Nizam's Dominions, but the bulk of its output goes West, and the coal supply of Madras is mainly obtained from Bengal either by rail or sea. The price of coal in Madras fluctuates considerably, and may be taken to average not less than Rs. 13 per ton. At one time wood was fairly cheap and was largely used for generating steam, but of late years the price has risen to from Rs. 11 to Rs. 13 a ton, and it is now mainly brought into Madras for domestic consumption, the average amount so used being about 110,000 tons per annum. In recent years very great improvements have been made in the methods of generating power, chiefly through the introduction of internal combustion engines, the advantages of which are most apparent when comparatively small amounts of power are required. The effect of this is beginning to be felt, which fact, combined with the present tendency of the educated classes of the country to turn their attention to industrial questions, has during the last few years induced a distinct movement in favour of industrial occupations. The material results so far achieved are not very important, but now that a start has been made, it can hardly be doubted that in time great changes will be effected.

In competition with the West, whilst India is at a disadvantage in many matters, it possesses an asset of enormous importance in its abundant supply of cheap labour. It is true that at the present time this labour is both unskilled and inefficient, but that this can be remedied by a practical system of industrial education has already been proved on a scale by no means insignificant. The results obtained in the mill industries, with labour still partially dependent upon agriculture, are no fair criterion by which to estimate the relative costs of labour in Eastern and Western countries. Far better results, though on a much smaller scale, have been obtained in factories which employ workmen who are artizans by caste, and possess a certain amount of hereditary aptitude for industrial work. In engineering shops, foundries and allied factories, although the workmen are still far below the standard of capacity to be found in England, yet under careful supervision they can be got to turn out thoroughly satisfactory work at a very much lower cost. In such shops the Indian workman earns about one-sixth of the pay, and does from one-third to one-half as much work as is the current practice in England, and is therefore a much cheaper workman.

The total population of Madras on the night of the Census was 518,660, and of these only 48,088 can be regarded as directly engaged in productive industrial work.

The following figures extracted from Table X of the Madras City Returns show in detail the number of persons engaged in the various industrial occupations pursued in the city :—

Description of occupation.	Workers.		
Class B.	Male.	Female.	Total.
Order VI. Textiles	10,800	1,136	11,936
" VII. Hides and skins, etc.	292	15	307
" VIII. Wood	4,399	144	4,543
" IX. Metals	3,306	43	3,349
" X. Ceramics	470	183	653
" XI. Chemical products, etc.	458	20	478
" XII. Food industries	1,478	2,694	4,172
" XIII. Industries of dress	5,163	772	5,935
" XIV. Furniture	150	9	159
" XV. Building industries	4,340	707	5,047
" XVI. Construction of means of transport	361	6	367
" XVII. Production and transformation of energy	369	13	382
" XVIII. Industries of luxury, printing, book-binding, jewellery and games	10,633	127	10,760
	42,219	5,869	48,088

From this it will be seen that there are 42,219 men and 5,869 women engaged in industries. Female labour is almost entirely confined to the textile trades, the food industries and those connected with clothing. The returns of building industries also include a considerable number of females who really belong to the cooly class, as their labour is entirely unskilled.

The next statement furnishes detailed information regarding the employment of labour in power factories :—

Industry.	Number of factories owned by				Number of managers who are		Persons employed.					
	Companies.	Individuals.		Total number.	Europeans or Anglo-Indians.	Indians.	Direction, etc.		Skilled workmen.		Unskilled workmen.	Total number.
		Europeans or Anglo-Indians.	Indians.				Europeans or Anglo-Indians.	Indians.	Europeans or Anglo-Indians.	Indians.		
1. Cotton Spinning Mills ...	1	...	...	1	...	1	...	18	...	417	86	521
2. Cotton Spinning and Weaving Mills	3	...	...	3	2	1	38	219	...	5,186	4,808	10,251
3. Iron and Steel Works ...	7	...	1	8	5	8	37	115	68	835	400	1,455
4. Aluminium Factory ...	1	...	...	1	1	...	5	12	4	186	54	261
5. Glass Works	1	...	...	1	1	...	2	3	2	11	4	22
6. Ærated Water Factories.	4	1	1	6	4	2	11	13	2	39	146	211
7. Oil Mills	...	...	2	2	...	2	...	66	...	82	42	190
8. Saw Mills	1	...	...	1	1	...	1	6	...	8	19	34
9. Bulk Oil Installations ...	4	...	...	4	4	...	1	25	1	220	175	422
10. Chemical Works (Medical Stores)	1	...	...	1	1	...	6	25	...	59	65	153
11. Rice Mills	...	...	2	2	...	2	...	3		11	81	95
12. Tanneries and Leather Trade Workshops ...	3	...	...	3	3	...	7	30	6	242	12	297
13. Cement Works	2	...	...	2	2	...	4	21	12	34	330	401
14. Electric Generating Stations	2	...	...	2	2	...	5	8	20	66	150	249
15. Printing Presses	16	...	7	23	10	13	52	397	58	3,820	771	5,098
16. Jewellery Workshops ...	1	...	...	1	1	...	10	37	5	208	31	291
17. Tobacco Factories ...	1	...	...	1	1	...	3	7	...	101	97	205
18. Garages	2	...	...	2	2	...	9	10	6	22	15	62
19. Coach Building Factories	3	...	...	3	2	1	4	51	...	316	119	490
20. Arsenal	...	...	...	...	1	...	41	44	10	281	391	767
Municipal Workshops ...	...	...	...	...	1	...	3	25	8	136	37	208
Locomotive running sheds	...	...	...	...	1	...	3	3	10	62	85	163
Tramway Workshops ...	...	...	...	...	1	...	3	11	1	158	120	93
Port Trust Workshops ...	...	...	...	...	3	...	23	20	98	467	908	1,516
Public Works Workshops and Stores	...	...	...	...	1	...	18	39	53	281	93	484
Total ...	...	...	...	...	50	25	286	1,208	364	13,247	9,039	24,144

The Census returns include a very large proportion of the employees of the locomotive workshops of the Madras and Southern Mahratta Railway, which lie outside the municipal limits to the north-west of Madras, and, at the same time, they do not include a considerable number of employees in the big cotton mills of Perambúr, who reside outside the muncipal limits. It is impossible, therefore, to state with any approach to accuracy the number of artizans working on their own account or associated in small groups. Roughly, however, the number may be taken at about 10,000, the bulk of whom are carpenters, metal-workers, jewellers and men engaged in the building trade.

Owing to differences in classification it has been found impossible to compare the numbers obtained in the Census of 1901 with the numbers obtained in the Census of 1911, except in a few cases which are given herewith :—

Number.	Occupation.	Workers.	
		1901.	1911.
1	Oil milling	219	250
2	Rice milling	3,605	1,888
3	Ærated water manufacture	46	74
4	Lime and cement manufacture	541	483
5	Cotton ginning	1,237	339
6	Cotton spinning and weaving in factories	2,950	5,878
7	Cotton weaving (hand)	3,990	3,958
8	Brass, copper and bell-metal workers	323	408
9	Carpenters	3,272	4,236
10	Shoe, boot and sandal makers	1,109	1,229
11	Jewellery	3,239	4,424

Examination of the statement will show that during the last ten years there have been considerable changes. There has been a great diminution in the number of rice pounders and huskers, doubtless owing to the large number of rice mills which have been established during the decade, so that rice instead of paddy is now brought into Madras. For reasons probably similar the amount of cotton ginning done in Madras has decreased to an even greater extent. During the last ten years only one cotton mill has been established, but there has been a considerable expansion in the output of those already established, necessitating a large increase in the number of people employed. It is interesting to note that the number of handloom weavers is practically the same as at the previous Census, and that apparently they are able to hold their own against the competition of power-loom factories. There has been some slight increase in the number of metal workers, and a considerable increase in the number of carpenters and jewellers, which may be taken as a not unfair indication of increased prosperity.

As might be expected in a capital city with a large population, there are a vast number of miscellaneous industries carried on, but none of them have obtained any considerable development and in the main they serve only to supply the local needs. The cost of living in Madras is distinctly higher than in other parts of the Presidency, and the pressure of foreign competition is therefore the more strongly felt by the indigenous artizans in the city than elsewhere. Moreover, in a seaport indigenous industries do not enjoy the small measure of protection afforded by the cost of transport to inland centres of population. It may be taken, therefore, as certain that the decay in the old industries of the country is more complete in Madras than elsewhere, and that the industrial future depends entirely upon the advantages offered by the city as a distributing centre for manufacture conducted on a large scale and on modern lines.

The next statement is a complete list of the organised industries using power in Madras and carried on in workshops employing more than twenty hands :—

	NO.
1. Cotton Mills	4
2. Iron Works	9
3. Engineering Shops— Public Works Department, Harbour, Municipal, South Indian Railway, Tramway Company, Arsenal	6
4. Electrical Generating Stations—	
Public	1
Private	7
5. Garages	3
6. Printing Presses	23
7. Tin-plate Works	2
8. Aluminium Works	1
9. Glass Works	1
10. Saw Mill	1
11. Baling Presses	4
12. Carpenter's Shops	7
13. Leather — Tannery	1
13. Leather — Warehouses	3
14. Technical and Industrial Education Workshops	3
15. Chemical Works	1
16. Rice Mills	2
17. Soda Water Factories	6
18. Ice Factories	2
19. Tobacco and Cigar Factory	1
20. Oil Mills	2
21. Bulk Oil Installations	4
22. Cement Works	2
23. Coach Builders	5
Total	101

By far the greater number of these are engaged in supplying the local needs of the community and are such as could be found in almost every large city : in fact, from an industrial point of view, only the four cotton mills, the cement works, two or three Iron Works and the aluminium factory are of commercial importance. The bulk oil installations, however, which do a very large business and are of great economic value, deserve attention. They are the direct outcome of the harbour works, without which it would have been impossible for them to have been established. During the last ten years the consumption of mineral oils has increased enormously in India and especially in the Madras Presidency, where very large quantities are now used in the numerous oil-engines which have been set up. In regard to the supply of liquid fuel, which is the residue left after the lighter oils have been distilled from crude petroleum, Madras compares not unfavourably with most other parts of the world which have not oil fields in their immediate neighbourhood. This is an industrial asset of no small importance, and will tend in the future to counterbalance largely the disadvantages, from which in other respects Madras suffers in the matter of fuel supply. Although there is only one tannery, and that of a specialised character, within the municipal limits, Madras is really a very important centre of the leather trade, and outside the municipal limits in the Chingleput district there are a large number of tanneries, mainly engaged in the preparation of hides and skins for export to Europe and America.

The following figures compiled from information kindly supplied by all the power users in Madras are interesting as showing the extent to which hand labour is assisted by modern methods of generating power :—

—	Number of engines.	Indicated or brake horse-power.	
Steam engines	63	13,250	I.H.P.
Gas engines	15	499	B.H.P.
Oil-engines	54	742	B.H.P.
Electric motors	104	534	B.H.P.

The figures for the horse-power are probably not very accurate, especially in respect to steam engines, many of which are old; and it will be safe to make a deduction of at least one-third to arrive at the actual horse-power daily generated. The cotton mills and the generating station of the Electric Supply Company account for the great bulk of the steam power. In all there are only 63 steam engines in Madras, as compared with 69 motors of the internal combustion type using either suction gas, liquid fuel, or kerosine oil. The latter have been installed within the last few years, and the extent to which power is now used to supplement hand-labour is shown by the fact that, in addition, 104 motors aggregating 534 horse-power have been attached to the mains of the Electric Supply Company. At 4 annas per kilowatt per hour the cost of power obtained in this way is very high, especially when allowance is made for the fact that small electric motors have a low efficiency. On a larger scale electric power is offered at somewhat lower rates, but for a steady load the terms offered are not sufficiently favourable to induce owners of generating plants to abandon them, or to prevent new private installations coming into existence. Nevertheless owing to the steadily increasing cost of labour an even more extended use of the facilities offered by the Electric Supply Company may be expected, whenever a very small or an intermittent supply of power is required. Ordinarily, however, except for very small units of power, or for supplies required intermittently, the use of internal combustion motors, whether worked by oil or gas, will be found more economical.

A careful scrutiny of the list of factories in Madras shows that in recent years only three new industries have been introduced into the city :—

(1) The manufacture of aluminium utensils now carried on by the Indian Aluminium Company.

(2) The manufacture of leather by the chrome tanning process carried on by Messrs. Chambers & Co.

(3) The manufacture of glass, chiefly sodawater bottles, by the Madras Glass Works.

The first two have passed the experimental stage and may be regarded as firmly established industries. In the older industries, there has been a considerable expansion in the outturn of the spinning and weaving mills, and a notable feature is the dye-houses attached to two of them. There has also been a considerable development in the engineering trades, consequent upon the extended use of motive power and machinery throughout the Presidency.

APPENDICES.

TABLE I.

Population by religions.

DIVISION.	NUMBER OF OCCUPIED HOUSES.	POPULATION.			HINDUS.			MUSALMANS.			CHRISTIANS.			OTHERS.		
		Persons.	Males.	Females.	Persons.	Males.	Females.	Persons.	Males.	Females.	Persons.	Males.	Females.	Persons.	Males.	Females.
1	2	3	4	5	6	7	8	9	10	11	12	13	14	15	16	17
I	3,396	20,318	9,768	10,550	13,976	6,861	7,115	1,015	490	525	5,271	2,392	2,879	56	25	31
II	6,223	40,635	20,396	20,239	36,276	18,182	18,094	3,196	1,633	1,563	1,151	573	578	12	8	4
III	2,356	15,120	7,820	7,300	12,502	6,512	5,990	2,193	1,072	1,121	327	185	142	98	51	47
IV	1,411	14,564	8,557	6,007	9,199	5,347	3,852	4,771	2,731	2,010	540	428	112	54	51	3
V	2,001	19,179	10,132	9,047	15,477	8,198	7,279	965	609	356	2,672	1,288	1,384	65	37	28
VI	2,210	22,473	12,027	10,446	15,951	8,240	7,711	4,087	2,291	1,796	2,421	1,483	938	14	13	1
VII	3,067	37,065	18,410	18,655	33,769	16,764	17,005	1,357	702	655	1,891	913	978	48	31	17
VIII	2,592	28,585	14,887	13,698	27,625	14,142	13,483	388	323	65	90	46	44	482	376	106
IX	1,757	20,937	11,210	9,727	19,634	10,425	9,209	276	221	55	962	505	457	65	59	6
X	3,376	24,979	13,137	11,842	18,981	9,982	8,999	5,139	2,703	2,436	815	425	390	44	27	17
XI	4,336	41,523	21,157	20,366	36,636	18,745	17,893	643	345	298	4,176	2,026	2,150	66	41	25
XII	2,868	29,776	15,172	14,604	22,629	11,566	11,063	1,798	1,085	713	5,144	2,384	2,760	205	137	68
XIII	2,863	23,717	12,430	11,287	17,399	9,240	8,159	2,053	1,160	893	4,176	1,979	2,197	89	51	38
XIV	2,264	11,751	6,216	5,535	10,105	5,295	4,810	270	183	87	1,372	734	638	4	4	...
XV	1,705	15,180	7,622	7,558	11,589	5,824	5,765	1,384	694	690	2,141	1,062	1,079	66	42	24
XVI	2,396	26,752	13,601	13,151	23,023	11,685	11,338	1,324	708	616	2,356	1,176	1,180	49	32	17
XVII	4,221	38,643	19,636	19,007	23,215	11,927	11,288	14,934	7,435	7,499	483	272	211	11	2	9
XVIII	3,604	32,851	16,724	16,127	24,738	12,762	11,976	7,490	3,636	3,854	572	298	274	51	28	23
XIX	4,382	34,358	16 998	17,360	26,006	12,960	13,046	5,274	2,630	2,644	2,806	1,267	1,539	272	141	131
XX	2,667	20,254	10,565	9,689	17,178	9,074	8,104	612	333	279	2,446	1,146	1,300	18	12	6
TOTAL ...	59,595	*518,660*	266,465	252,195	*415,910*	213,731	202,179	*59,169*	30,984	28,185	*41,812*	20,582	21,230	* *1,769*	1,168	601

* Made up of 954 Jains (Males 699, Females 255), 532 Buddhists (M. 323, F. 209), 146 Parsis (M. 66, F. 80), 113 Brahmos (M. 66, F. 47), 16 Jews (M. 10, F. 6) and eight Atheists (M. 4, F. 4).

TABLE II.

Variation in Population since 1891.

DIVISION.	PERSONS.			MALES.			FEMALES.			Variation increase (+) or decrease (−).			Percentage Variation.			Number of females to 1,000 males.		
	1911.	1901.	1891.	1911.	1901.	1891.	1911.	1901.	1891	1901 to 1911.	1891 to 1901.	1891 to 1911.	1901 to 1911.	1891 to 1901.	1891 to 1911.	1911.	1901.	1891.
1	2	3	4	5	6	7	8	9	10	11	12	13	14	15	16	17	18	19
I	20,318	21,190	21,705	9,768	10,308	10,637	10,550	10,882	11,068	− 872	− 515	− 1,387	− 4·1	− 2·4	− 6·4	1,080	1,056	1,041
II	40,635	46,512	36,984	20,396	22,923	18,115	20,239	23,589	18,869	− 5,877	+ 9,528	+ 3,651	− 12·6	+ 25·8	+ 9·9	992	1,029	1,042
III	15,120	16,454	13,086	7,820	8,433	6,472	7,300	8,021	6,614	− 1,334	+ 3,368	+ 2,034	− 8·1	+ 25·7	+ 15·5	934	951	1,022
IV	14,564	17,856	12,017	8,557	9,770	6,503	6,007	8,086	5,514	− 3,292	+ 5,839	+ 2,547	− 18·4	+ 48·6	+ 21·2	702	828	848
V	19,179	17,557	20,409	10,132	8,828	10,129	9,047	8,729	10,280	+ 1,622	− 2,852	− 1,230	+ 9·2	− 14·0	− 6·0	893	989	1,015
VI	22,473	26,550	27,031	12,027	14,014	13,688	10,446	12,536	13,343	− 4,077	− 481	− 4,558	− 15·3	− 1·8	− 16·9	869	895	975
VII	37,065	38,403	36,287	18,410	18,881	17,732	18,655	19,522	18,555	− 1,338	+ 2,116	+ 778	− 3·5	+ 5·8	+ 2·1	1,013	1,034	1,046
VIII	28,585	28,668	26,462	14,887	14,366	13,204	13,698	14,302	13,258	− 83	+ 2,206	+ 2,123	− 0·3	+ 8·3	+ 8·0	920	996	1,004
IX	20,937	22,304	21,636	11,210	11,506	11,069	9,727	10,798	10,567	− 1,367	+ 668	− 699	− 6·1	+ 3·1	− 3·2	868	938	955
X	24,979	23,223	17,488	13,137	12,328	9,065	11,842	10,895	8,423	+ 1,756	+ 5,735	+ 7,491	+ 7·6	+ 32·8	+ 42·8	901	884	929
XI	41,523	37,106	30,965	21,157	18,645	15,328	20,366	18,461	15,637	+ 4,417	+ 6,141	+ 10,558	+ 11·9	+ 19·8	+ 34·1	963	990	1,020
XII	29,776	26,960	24,499	15,172	13,279	12,456	14,604	13,681	12,043	+ 2,816	+ 2,461	+ 5,277	+ 10·4	+ 10·0	+ 21·5	963	1,030	967
XIII	23,717	21,954	18,084	12,430	11,543	8,829	11,287	10,411	9,255	+ 1,763	+ 3,870	+ 5,633	+ 8·0	+ 21·4	+ 31·1	908	902	1,048
XIV	11,751	9,546	8,880	6,216	4,724	4,420	5,535	4,822	4,460	+ 2,205	+ 666	+ 2,871	+ 23·1	+ 7·5	+ 32·3	890	1,021	1,009
XV	15,180	14,297	12,710	7,622	7,044	6,143	7,558	7,253	6,567	+ 883	+ 1,587	+ 2,470	+ 6·2	+ 12·5	+ 19·4	992	1,030	1,069
XVI	26,752	26,624	22,823	13,601	13,287	11,382	13,151	13,337	11,441	+ 128	+ 3,801	+ 3,929	+ 0·5	+ 16·7	+ 17·2	967	1,004	1,005
XVII	38,643	35,779	29,970	19,636	17,769	14,573	19,007	18,010	15,397	+ 2,864	+ 5,809	+ 8,673	+ 8·0	+ 19·4	+ 28·9	968	1,014	1,057
XVIII	32,851	31,451	28,495	16,724	15,784	14,141	16,127	15,667	14,354	+ 1,400	+ 2,956	+ 4,356	+ 4·5	+ 10·4	+ 15·3	964	993	1,015
XIX	34,358	30,114	26,057	16,998	14,859	12,781	17,360	15,255	13,276	+ 4,244	+ 4,057	+ 8,301	+ 14·1	+ 15·6	+ 31·9	1,021	1,027	1,039
XX	20,254	16,798	15,052	10,565	8,439	7,574	9,689	8,359	7,478	+ 3,456	+ 1,746	+ 5,202	+ 20·6	+ 11·6	+ 34·6	917	991	987
MISCELLANEOUS ...	...	...	1,878	...	...	1,576	...	...	302	...	− 1,878	− 1,878	...	...	...	...	...	192
TOTAL ...	*518,660*	509,346	452,518	*266,465*	256,730	225,817	*252,195*	252,616	226,701	+ *9,314*	+ 56,828	+ 66,142	+ *1·8*	+ 12·6	+ 14·6	*946*	984	1,004

1-A

TABLE III.

Age, Sex and Civil Condition—All Religions (All divisions).

AGE.	POPULATION.			UNMARRIED.			MARRIED.			WIDOWED.		
	Persons.	Males.	Females.	Persons.	Males.	Females.	Persons.	Males.	Females.	Persons.	Males.	Females.
1	2	3	4	5	6	7	8	9	10	11	12	13
0–1	13,134	6,502	6,632	13,110	6,491	6,619	24	11	13	...	...	...
1–2	6,811	3,388	3,423	6,799	3,383	3,416	12	5	7	...	...	...
2–3	12,150	5,983	6,167	12,117	5,971	6,146	28	10	18	5	2	3
3–4	13,475	6,631	6,844	13,441	6,617	6,824	30	14	16	4	...	4
4–5	11,451	5,732	5,719	11,407	5,711	5,696	33	19	14	11	2	9
0–5	*57,021*	28,236	28,785	*56,874*	28,173	28,701	*127*	59	68	*20*	4	16
5–10	57,640	28,650	28,990	57,124	28,542	28,582	488	101	387	28	7	21
10–15	52,816	27,709	25,107	47,952	27,384	20,568	4,763	319	4,444	101	6	95
15–20	50,867	24,935	25,932	29,017	22,438	6,579	21,193	2,471	18,722	657	26	631
20–25	55,099	28,158	26,941	18,684	16,539	2,145	34,547	11,397	23,150	1,868	222	1,646
25–30	50,006	25,789	24,217	7,799	6,698	1,101	39,161	18,551	20,610	3,046	540	2,506
30–35	43,517	22,464	21,053	3,074	2,410	664	35,780	19,252	16,528	4,663	802	3,861
35–40	33,804	18,716	15,088	1,656	1,203	453	27,068	16,576	10,492	5,080	937	4,143
40–45	35,288	18,716	16,572	1,070	720	350	25,934	16,703	9,231	8,284	1,293	6,991
45–50	22,424	12,153	10,271	590	406	184	15,128	10,580	4,548	6,706	1,167	5,539
50–55	23,215	11,888	11,327	465	293	172	13,568	10,027	3,541	9,182	1,568	7,614
55–60	10,993	5,874	5,119	239	164	75	5,849	4,716	1,133	4,905	994	3,911
60–65	14,070	7,145	6,925	226	155	71	6,347	5,380	967	7,497	1,610	5,887
65–70	4,430	2,375	2,055	99	66	33	1,875	1,652	223	2,456	657	1,799
70 and over	7,470	3,657	3,813	137	94	43	2,529	2,333	196	4,804	1,230	3,574
TOTAL ...	*518,660*	266,465	252,195	*225,006*	135,285	89,721	*234,357*	120,117	114,240	*59,297*	11,063	48,234

TABLE III.

Age, Sex and Civil Condition (All divisions).

AGE.	HINDUS.												MUSALMANS.					
	POPULATION.			UNMARRIED.			MARRIED.			WIDOWED.			POPULATION.			UNMARRIED.		
	Total.	Males.	Females.	Total.	Males.	Females.	Total.	Males.	Females.	Total.	Males.	Females.	Total.	Males.	Females.	Total.	Males.	Females.
1	2	3	4	5	6	7	8	9	10	11	12	13	14	15	16	17	18	19
0-1	10,543	5,197	5,346	10,519	5,186	5,333	24	11	13	...	...	...	1,394	696	698	1,394	696	698
1-2	5,537	2,761	2,776	5,528	2,756	2,772	9	5	4	...	...	...	645	305	340	642	305	337
2-3	9,817	4,763	5,054	9,790	4,754	5,036	22	7	15	5	2	3	1,331	716	615	1,325	713	612
3-4	11,011	5,432	5,579	10,981	5,418	5,563	26	14	12	4	...	4	1,382	674	708	1,378	674	704
4-5	9,161	4,547	4,614	9,123	4,528	4,595	28	17	11	10	2	8	1,374	699	675	1,369	697	672
5—10	45,705	22,663	23,042	45,237	22,575	22,662	446	82	364	22	6	16	6,890	3,512	3,378	6,847	3,494	3,353
10—15	41,427	21,884	19,543	37,041	21,620	15,421	4,296	259	4,037	90	5	85	6,482	3,449	3,033	6,084	3,410	2,674
15—20	40,473	19,897	20,576	21,659	17,616	4,043	18,259	2,258	16,001	555	23	532	5,762	2,945	2,817	3,576	2,782	794
20—25	44,204	22,561	21,643	13,596	12,404	1,192	29,034	9,962	19,072	1,574	195	1,379	6,146	3,143	3,003	2,373	2,198	175
25—30	40,276	20,773	19,503	5,436	4,769	667	32,306	15,563	16,743	2,534	441	2,093	5,408	2,750	2,658	937	888	49
30—35	35,450	18,445	17,005	2,119	1,744	375	29,392	16,030	13,362	3,939	671	3,268	4,907	2,457	2,450	344	296	48
35—40	27,420	15,268	12,152	1,134	866	268	23,116	13,656	8,460	4,170	746	3,424	3,508	1,992	1,516	148	125	23
40—45	28,828	15,287	13,541	764	530	234	21,115	13,684	7,431	6,949	1,073	5,876	4,021	2,154	1,867	89	73	16
45—50	18,102	9,757	8,345	383	278	105	12,128	8,506	3,622	5,591	973	4,618	2,372	1,381	991	48	42	6
50—55	18,810	9,534	9,276	320	216	104	10,864	8,032	2,832	7,626	1,286	6,340	2,800	1,557	1,243	39	31	8
55—60	8,825	4,692	4,133	152	113	39	4,645	3,752	893	4,028	827	3,201	1,182	677	505	19	14	5
60—65	11,232	5,693	5,539	158	111	47	4,958	4,223	735	6,116	1,359	4,757	1,897	984	913	23	22	1
65—70	3,410	1,813	1,597	54	38	16	1,421	1,251	170	1,935	524	1,411	533	310	223	9	7	2
70 and over ...	5,679	2,764	2,915	90	69	21	1,900	1,751	149	3,689	944	2,745	1,135	588	552	12	12	...
TOTAL ...	*415,910*	213,731	202,179	*174,064*	105,591	68,493	*192,989*	99,063	93,926	*48,837*	9,077	39,760	*59,169*	30,984	28,185	*26,656*	16,479	10,177

TABLE III.

Age, Sex and Civil Condition (All divisions)—*continued.*

AGE.	MUSALMANS—*cont.* Married. Total	Married. Males.	Married. Females.	Widowed. Total.	Widowed. Males.	Widowed. Females.	CHRISTIANS. Population. Total.	Population. Males.	Population. Females.	Unmarried. Total.	Unmarried. Males.	Unmarried. Females.	Married. Total	Married. Males.	Married. Females.	Widowed. Total.	Widowed. Males.	Widowed. Females.
	20	21	22	23	24	25	26	27	28	29	30	31	32	33	34	35	36	37
0-1	...	...	...	...	...	...	1,161	591	570	1,161	591	570	...	...	..	...	..	...
1-2	3	...	3	...	...	...	618	318	300	618	318	300	...	...	...	...	...	...
2-3	6	3	3	..	...	...	975	490	485	975	490	485	...	...	...	...	...	...
3-4	4	...	4	...	...	...	1,052	508	544	1,052	508	544	..	...	...	...	...	...
4-5	5	2	3	...	...	...	894	476	418	894	476	418	...	..	...	...	...	...
5-10	38	17	21	5	1	4	4,887	2,398	2,489	4,887	2,398	2,489	..	..	...	...	...	...
10-15	390	39	351	8	...	8	4,742	2,266	2,476	4,676	2,254	2,422	64	12	52	2	...	2
15-20	2,108	161	1,947	78	2	76	4,394	1,921	2,473	3,626	1,902	1,724	745	18	727	23	1	22
20-25	3,581	925	2,656	192	20	172	4,508	2,275	2,233	2,608	1,834	774	1,805	436	1,369	95	5	90
25-30	4,158	1,799	2,359	313	63	250	4,107	2,117	1,990	1,384	1,002	382	2,538	1,085	1,453	185	30	155
30-35	4,107	2,074	2,033	456	87	369	2,986	1,444	1,542	593	355	238	2,136	1,050	1,086	257	39	218
35-40	2,863	1,759	1,104	497	108	389	2,742	1,357	1,385	363	202	161	1,980	1,078	902	399	77	322
40-45	3,099	1,970	1,129	833	111	722	2,316	1,189	1,127	208	110	98	1,618	973	645	490	106	384
45-50	1,705	1,244	461	619	95	524	1,877	969	908	153	81	72	1,249	795	454	475	93	382
50-55	1,804	1,377	427	957	149	808	1,545	763	782	105	45	60	863	590	273	577	128	449
55-60	699	585	114	464	78	386	957	486	471	67	36	31	485	363	122	405	87	318
60-65	960	818	142	914	144	770	923	460	463	45	22	23	422	334	88	456	104	352
65-70	265	245	20	259	58	201	480	248	232	36	21	15	184	152	32	260	75	185
70 and over ...	441	409	32	682	162	520	648	306	342	34	12	22	187	172	15	427	122	305
TOTAL ...	*26,236*	13,427	12,809	*6,277*	1,078	5,199	*41,812*	20,582	21,230	*23,465*	12,657	10,828	*14,276*	7,058	7,218	*4,051*	867	3,184

TABLE III.

Age, Sex and Civil Condition (by divisions)—HINDUS (MALE).

DIVISION.	TOTAL.				0—5.				5—10.				10—15.			
	Total.	Unmarried.	Married.	Widowed.	Total.	Unmarried.	Married.	Widowed.	Total.	Unmarried.	Married.	Widowed.	Total.	Unmarried.	Married.	Widowed.
1	2	3	4	5	6	7	8	9	10	11	12	13	14	15	16	17
I	6,861	3,421	3,168	272	874	870	3	1	859	851	8	...	701	696	5	...
II	18,182	8,433	8,901	848	2,168	2,168	...	...	1,832	1,832	...	...	1,715	1,697	17	1
III	6,512	3,217	2,991	304	752	747	5	...	672	669	3	...	673	668	5	...
IV	5,347	2,282	2,869	196	404	401	3	...	360	357	3	...	379	372	7	...
V	8,198	3,754	4,134	310	706	706	...	...	685	685	...	...	857	841	16	...
VI	8,240	3,849	3,964	427	683	683	...	...	774	769	5	...	781	769	12	...
VII	16,764	8,234	7,696	834	1,570	1,569	1	...	1,699	1,690	6	3	1,721	1,707	13	1
VIII	14,142	6,670	6,805	667	1,173	1,167	4	2	1,284	1,282	2	...	1,457	1,428	29	...
IX	10,425	4,677	5,285	463	902	898	4	...	913	908	4	1	1,019	996	23	...
X	9,982	5,305	4,309	368	1,217	1,209	8	...	1,175	1,171	4	...	1,122	1,113	9	..
XI	18,745	9,717	8,203	825	2,048	2,038	9	1	2,062	2,046	15	1	2,088	2,062	26	...
XII	11,566	6,119	5,028	419	1,287	1,287	...	...	1,339	1,339	...	...	1,274	1,260	12	2
XIII	9,240	4,759	4,171	310	978	978	...	...	1,036	1,036	...	...	839	833	6	...
XIV	5,295	2,647	2,268	380	666	665	1	...	586	578	8	...	479	473	6	...
XV	5,824	3,056	2,543	225	729	729	...	...	735	733	2	...	623	614	8	1
XVI	11,685	6,071	5,187	427	1,346	1,339	7	...	1,379	1,369	9	1	1,259	1,248	11	...
XVII	11,927	5,990	5,522	415	1,274	1,265	9	...	1,344	1,338	6	...	1,175	1,158	17	...
XVIII	12,762	6,164	6,077	521	1,340	1,340	...	...	1,356	1,356	...	...	1,334	1,327	7	...
XIX	12,960	6,615	5,818	527	1,527	1,527	...	...	1,554	1,554	...	...	1,389	1,381	8	...
XX	9,074	4,611	4,124	339	1,056	1,056	...	...	1,019	1,012	7	...	999	977	22	...
TOTAL ...	*213,731*	*105,591*	*99,063*	*9,077*	*22,700*	22,642	54	4	*22,663*	22,575	82	6	*21,884*	21,620	259	5

TABLE III.

Age, Sex and Civil Condition (by divisions)—HINDUS (MALE)—*continued.*

DIVISION.	15—20.				20—40.				40—55.				55—70.				70 and over.			
	Total.	Unmarried.	Married.	Widowed.	Total.	Unmarried.	Married.	Widowed.	Total.	Unmarried.	Married.	Widowed.	Total.	Unmarried.	Married.	Widowed.	Total.	Unmarried.	Married.	Widowed.
	18	19	20	21	22	23	24	25	26	27	28	29	30	31	32	33	34	35	36	37
I	521	473	48	...	2,241	507	1,671	63	1,159	20	1,042	97	404	3	316	85	102	1	75	26
II	1,450	1,305	140	5	6,499	1,331	4,962	206	3,238	75	2,852	311	1,037	20	786	231	243	5	144	94
III	558	512	41	...	2,266	580	1,614	72	1,138	34	991	113	379	6	278	95	79	1	54	24
IV	584	466	117	1	2,490	649	1,800	41	808	27	726	55	253	8	181	64	69	2	32	35
V	835	682	153	...	3,355	785	2,483	87	1,284	46	1,121	117	414	7	324	83	62	2	37	23
VI	763	686	77	...	3,290	896	2,283	111	1,427	40	1,232	155	409	4	291	114	113	2	64	47
VII	1,579	1,417	161	1	6,181	1,744	4,236	201	2,860	83	2,457	320	960	22	708	230	194	2	114	78
VIII	1,377	1,174	200	3	5,559	1,512	3,895	152	2,415	80	2,060	275	733	21	522	190	144	6	93	45
IX	1,002	838	162	2	4,036	931	2,994	111	1,815	77	1,558	180	625	26	469	130	113	3	71	39
X	892	821	70	1	3,283	939	2,277	67	1,545	37	1,382	126	568	11	446	111	180	4	113	63
XI	1,852	1,712	137	3	6,233	1,750	4,324	159	2,993	74	2,620	299	1,212	20	905	287	257	15	167	75
XII	1,144	1,049	95	...	4,065	1,132	2,838	95	1,697	40	1,507	150	632	9	493	130	128	3	83	42
XIII	784	710	72	2	3,545	1,114	2,371	60	1,431	75	1,256	100	501	11	384	106	126	2	82	42
XIV	417	372	45	...	1,845	505	1,249	91	896	40	692	164	339	13	226	100	67	1	41	25
XV	503	467	36	...	1,862	486	1,323	53	919	23	818	78	364	4	295	65	89	...	61	28
XVI	1,083	994	88	1	4,009	1,053	2,860	96	1,838	48	1,626	164	617	15	483	119	154	5	103	46
XVII	1,245	1,060	185	...	4,335	1,091	3,143	101	1,690	55	1.487	148	689	18	550	121	175	5	125	45
XVIII	1,287	1,080	207	...	4,533	979	3,428	126	1,997	55	1,766	176	760	22	576	162	155	5	93	57
XIX	1,119	1,019	98	2	4,351	1,076	3,187	88	2,082	47	1,847	188	756	9	557	190	182	2	121	59
XX	907	779	126	2	3,069	723	2,273	73	1,346	48	1,182	116	546	13	436	97	132	3	78	51
TOTAL ...	*19,897*	17,616	2,258	23	*77,047*	19,783	55,211	2,053	*34,578*	1,024	30,222	3,332	*12,196*	262	9,226	2,710	*2,764*	69	1,751	944

TABLE III.

Age, Sex and Civil Condition (by divisions)—HINDUS (FEMALE).

DIVISION.	TOTAL.				0—5.				5—10.				10—15.			
	Total.	Unmarried.	Married.	Widowed.	Total.	Unmarried.	Married.	Widowed.	Total.	Unmarried.	Married.	Widowed.	Total.	Unmarried.	Married.	Widowed.
1	2	3	4	5	6	7	8	9	10	11	12	13	14	15	16	17
I	7,115	2,672	3,232	1,211	972	970	2	...	887	872	15	...	622	535	85	2
II	18,094	5,701	8,978	3,415	2,116	2,116	...	...	2,006	1,988	18	...	1,517	1,172	340	5
III	5,990	2,009	2,773	1,208	713	708	5	...	655	640	15	...	563	460	101	2
IV	3,852	1,109	1,906	837	370	370	...	...	353	339	12	2	330	253	75	2
V	7,279	2,312	3,482	1,485	730	726	4	...	707	698	9	...	707	516	191	...
VI	7,711	2,213	3,647	1,851	714	714	...	...	739	731	8	..	717	553	164	...
VII	17,005	5,483	7,848	3,674	1,663	1,658	5	...	1,767	1,751	15	1	1,740	1,438	291	11
VIII	13,483	4,063	6,291	3,129	1,217	1,210	6	1	1,299	1,274	25	...	1,246	906	333	7
IX	9,209	2,739	4,495	1,975	944	943	...	1	905	887	17	1	884	636	241	7
X	8,999	3,348	4,125	1,526	1,227	1,220	4	3	1,191	1,169	21	1	832	658	172	2
XI	17,893	6,295	8,273	3,325	2,148	2,133	11	4	2,173	2,139	32	2	1,809	1,499	305	5
XII	11,063	4,101	4,846	2,116	1,411	1,411	...	...	1,349	1,327	22	...	1,121	899	216	6
XIII	8,159	3,056	3,637	1,466	1,055	1,055	...	...	1,045	1,029	16	...	817	662	146	9
XIV	4,810	1,719	2,153	938	657	656	1	...	554	542	10	2	427	337	86	4
XV	5,765	2,230	2,544	991	735	735	...	...	745	736	9	...	610	523	87	...
XVI	11,338	4,164	5,094	2,080	1,443	1,429	9	5	1,390	1,367	21	2	1,119	903	209	7
XVII	11,288	3,872	5,233	2,183	1,313	1,305	8	...	1,332	1,308	22	2	1,120	888	226	6
XVIII	11,976	3,705	5,753	2,518	1,298	1,297	...	1	1,351	1,319	31	1	1,189	825	361	3
XIX	13,046	4,889	5,779	2,378	1,619	1,619	...	...	1,606	1,584	22	...	1,365	1,154	211	...
XX	8,104	2,813	3,837	1,454	1,024	1,024	...	...	988	962	24	2	808	604	197	7
TOTAL ...	202,179	68,493	93,926	39,760	23,369	23,299	55	15	23,042	22,662	364	16	19,543	15,421	4,087	85

TABLE III.

Age, Sex and Civil Condition (by divisions)—HINDUS (FEMALE)—*continued.*

DIVISION.	15—20.				20—40.				40—55.				55—70.				70 and over.			
	Total.	Unmarried.	Married.	Widowed.	Total.	Unmarried.	Married.	Widowed.	Total.	Unmarried.	Married.	Widowed.	Total.	Unmarried.	Married.	Widowed.	Total.	Unmarried.	Married.	Widowed.
	18	19	20	21	22	23	24	25	26	27	28	29	30	31	32	33	34	35	36	37
I	648	166	462	20	2,456	108	2,081	267	1,005	16	499	490	431	5	82	344	94	...	6	88
II	1,867	275	1,551	41	6,678	125	5,633	920	2,767	17	1,282	1,468	901	6	137	758	242	2	17	223
III	626	123	486	17	2,059	70	1,703	286	965	6	403	556	330	2	56	272	79	...	4	75
IV	440	68	360	12	1,448	64	1,180	204	626	11	247	368	222	4	29	189	63	...	3	60
V	813	157	630	26	2,703	161	2,110	432	1,129	43	477	609	412	7	59	346	78	4	2	72
VI	818	134	650	34	2,890	66	2,310	514	1,300	13	456	831	427	1	57	369	106	1	2	103
VII	1,766	371	1,352	43	6,141	207	4,936	998	2,737	47	1,119	1,571	942	10	122	810	249	1	8	240
VIII	1,427	252	1,147	28	5,002	314	3,803	885	2,309	86	868	1,355	807	19	100	688	176	2	9	165
IX	956	128	800	28	3,355	112	2,708	535	1,571	27	652	892	474	4	74	396	120	2	3	115
X	863	177	665	21	3,004	108	2,539	357	1,303	14	637	652	452	2	80	370	127	...	7	120
XI	1,814	333	1,443	38	6,004	163	5,031	810	2,723	24	1,259	1,440	979	4	177	798	243	...	15	228
XII	1,178	268	876	34	3,671	169	2,938	564	1,565	20	695	850	633	7	93	533	135	...	6	129
XIII	846	199	625	22	2,713	101	2,220	392	1,100	7	533	560	468	3	89	376	115	...	8	107
XIV	350	126	217	7	1,758	49	1,458	251	703	6	321	376	293	1	58	234	68	2	2	64
XV	552	153	385	14	1,820	72	1,518	230	913	9	479	425	302	2	58	242	88	...	8	80
XVI	1,139	256	857	26	3,725	182	3,098	445	1,696	20	787	889	651	4	101	546	175	3	12	160
XVII	1,169	240	899	30	3,770	104	3,140	526	1,720	20	815	885	667	7	114	546	197	...	9	188
XVIII	1,242	176	1,035	31	3,961	63	3,290	608	1,976	19	920	1,037	704	4	108	592	255	2	8	245
XIX	1,208	296	875	37	4,473	205	3,679	589	1,875	24	851	1,000	704	5	126	573	196	2	15	179
XX	854	145	686	23	2,672	59	2,262	351	1,179	14	585	580	470	5	78	387	109	...	5	104
TOTAL ...	*20,576*	4,043	16,001	532	*70,303*	2,502	57,637	10,164	*31,162*	443	13,885	16,834	*11,269*	102	1,798	9,369	*2,915*	21	149	2,745

TABLE III.

Age, Sex and Civil Condition (by divisions)—MUSALMANS (MALE).

DIVISION.	TOTAL.				0—5.				5—10.				10—15.			
	Total.	Unmarried.	Married.	Widowed.	Total.	Unmarried.	Married.	Widowed.	Total.	Unmarried.	Married.	Widowed.	Total.	Unmarried.	Married.	Widowed.
1	2	3	4	5	6	7	8	9	10	11	12	13	14	15	16	17
I	490	237	240	13	46	45	1	...	67	67	...	...	56	56	...	...
II	1,633	828	744	61	178	178	...	...	195	195	...	...	156	154	2	...
III	1,072	557	477	38	114	114	...	...	119	117	2	...	133	133	...	...
IV	2,731	1,336	1,324	71	234	234	...	...	248	246	2	...	244	243	1	...
V	609	303	285	21	40	40	...	...	36	36	...	...	48	48	...	...
VI	2,291	1,198	1,015	78	187	187	...	...	227	227	...	...	253	253	...	...
VII	702	359	316	27	79	79	...	...	76	76	...		72	71	1	...
VIII	323	175	143	5	9	9	...	...	9	9	...	...	19	19	...	...
IX	221	74	141	6	8	8	...	...	5	5	...	...	12	12	...	...
X	2,703	1,565	1,043	95	292	289	3	...	347	341	5	1	365	359	6	...
XI	345	172	162	11	41	41	...	...	29	29	...	...	28	27	1	...
XII	1,085	555	502	28	97	97	...	...	97	97		...	103	99	4	...
XIII	1,160	583	545	32	109	109	...	...	114	114	...	...	109	109	...	...
XIV	183	72	64	47	14	14	...	...	13	13	...	...	12	11	1	...
XV	694	382	284	28	69	69	...	...	93	93	...	...	90	86	4	...
XVI	708	395	286	27	95	95	...	...	75	72	3	...	75	72	3	...
XVII	7,435	4,102	3,071	262	775	774	1	...	910	906	4	...	873	866	7	...
XVIII	3,636	1,982	1,540	114	387	387	...	...	476	476	...	...	472	465	7	...
XIX	2,630	1,433	1,095	102	296	296	...	...	342	342	...	...	287	287	...	...
XX	333	171	150	12	20	20	...		34	33	1	...	42	40	2	...
TOTAL ...	*30,984*	*16,479*	*13,427*	*1,078*	*3,090*	3,085	5	...	*3,512*	3,494	17	1	*3,449*	3,410	39	...

TABLE III.

Age, Sex and Civil Condition (by divisions)—MUSALMANS (MALE)—*continued.*

DIVISION.	15—20				20—40				40—55				55—70				70 and over			
	Total.	Unmarried.	Married.	Widowed.	Total.	Unmarried.	Married.	Widowed.	Total.	Unmarried.	Married.	Widowed.	Total.	Unmarried.	Married.	Widowed.	Total.	Unmarried.	Married.	Widowed.
	18	19	20	21	22	23	24	25	26	27	28	29	30	31	32	33	34	35	36	37
I	36	35	1	...	135	33	99	3	97	...	94	3	39	...	34	5	14	1	11	2
II	136	130	6	...	545	164	363	18	289	7	260	22	110	...	94	16	24	...	19	5
III	99	91	8	...	321	94	218	9	190	7	166	17	77	1	70	6	19	...	13	6
IV	253	236	17	...	1,088	354	720	14	464	20	418	26	159	3	133	23	41	...	33	8
V	79	79	...	...	282	96	181	5	94	2	83	9	25	1	19	5	5	1	2	2
VI	267	242	25	...	883	276	580	27	335	10	307	18	114	2	86	26	25	1	17	7
VII	60	56	4	...	238	71	157	10	127	4	117	6	37	2	30	5	13	...	7	6
VIII	52	52	...	...	170	83	84	3	51	2	47	2	8	1	7	...	5	...	5	...
IX	14	13	1	...	123	34	86	3	48	2	45	1	11	...	9	2	...	...	...	...
X	268	253	15	...	745	307	423	15	469	12	423	34	181	4	146	31	36	...	22	14
XI	30	29	1	...	133	46	85	2	54	...	50	4	24	.	23	1	6	...	2	4
XII	126	120	6	...	433	140	287	6	146	2	135	9	63	...	53	10	20	...	17	3
XIII	91	86	5	...	439	150	279	10	221	8	203	10	63	6	49	8	14	1	9	4
XIV	6	5	1	...	69	21	30	18	47	4	20	23	17	4	9	4	5	...	3	2
XV	65	64	1	...	212	67	138	7	87	3	78	6	65	...	56	9	13	...	7	6
XVI	74	72	2	...	205	80	122	3	127	4	113	10	50	...	39	11	7	...	4	3
XVII	668	638	28	2	2,343	870	1,399	74	1,207	35	1,097	75	466	8	403	55	193	5	132	56
XVIII	342	321	21	...	1,090	315	752	23	526	12	479	35	261	5	218	38	82	1	63	18
XIX	246	230	16	...	778	263	492	23	452	9	405	38	176	4	147	25	53	2	35	16
XX	33	30	3	...	110	43	62	5	61	3	51	7	25	2	23	...	8	...	8	...
TOTAL ...	*2,945*	2,782	161	2	*10,342*	3,507	6,557	278	*5,092*	146	4,591	355	*1,971*	43	1,648	280	*583*	12	409	162

TABLE III.

Age, Sex and Civil Condition (by divisions)—MUSALMANS (FEMALE).

DIVISION.	TOTAL.				0–5.				5–10.				10–15.			
	Total.	Unmarried.	Married.	Widowed.	Total.	Unmarried.	Married.	Widowed.	Total.	Unmarried.	Married.	Widowed.	Total.	Unmarried.	Married.	Widowed.
1	2	3	4	5	6	7	8	9	10	11	12	13	14	15	16	17
I	525	118	291	116	39	39	..	...	50	50	...	...	35	24	11	...
II	1,563	534	729	300	168	168	...	...	192	191	1	...	162	138	24	...
III	1,121	371	526	224	116	116	...	...	137	134	2	1	122	96	26	...
IV	2,040	680	982	378	218	218	...	...	221	221	...	...	203	184	19	...
V	356	120	167	69	38	38	...	...	30	30		...	39	35	4	...
VI	1,796	620	853	323	192	192	...	...	201	201	...	...	180	162	18	...
VII	655	200	316	139	61	61	...	...	61	61	...	...	55	50	4	1
VIII	65	25	30	10	11	11	...	...	9	9	...	...	3	3		...
IX	55	16	29	10	6	5	1	...	6	5	1	...	7	5	2	...
X	2,436	929	1,050	457	299	295	4	...	328	321	7	...	292	249	42	1
XI	298	110	139	49	39	39	...	...	35	35	...	...	33	26	7	...
XII	713	247	329	137	84	84	...	...	82	82	..	..	70	58	12	...
XIII	893	347	421	125	114	114	...	...	119	118	1	...	88	82	6	...
XIV	87	22	45	20	8	8	...	...	12	11	1	..	3	1	2	..
XV	690	273	284	133	80	80	...	...	74	74	...	...	93	84	9	...
XVI	616	221	281	114	61	61	...	...	79	79	...	...	65	54	10	1
XVII	7,499	2,778	3,346	1,375	752	744	8	...	899	888	8	3	843	773	68	2
XVIII	3,854	1,440	1,703	711	412	412	...	...	483	483	...	...	420	363	57	...
XIX	2,644	1,013	1,170	461	308	308	...	...	335	335	...	...	285	255	27	3
XX	279	113	118	48	30	30	...	...	25	25	...	...	35	32	3	...
TOTAL ...	28,185	10,177	12,809	5,199	3,036	3,023	13	...	3,378	3,353	21	4	3,033	2,674	351	8

TABLE III.

Age, Sex and Civil Condition (by divisions) -MUSALMANS (FEMALE)-*continued.*

DIVISION.	15–20.				20–40.				40–55.				55–70.				70 and over.			
	Total.	Unmarried.	Married.	Widowed.	Total.	Unmarried.	Married.	Widowed.	Total.	Unmarried.	Married.	Widowed.	Total.	Unmarried.	Married.	Widowed.	Total.	Unmarried.	Married.	Widowed.
	18	19	20	21	22	23	24	25	26	[illegible]	28	29	30	31	32	33	34	35	36	37
I	56	1	52	3	194	4	172	18	87	...	47	40	50	...	8	42	14	...	1	13
II	167	30	132	5	550	6	460	84	212	1	100	111	77	...	10	67	35	...	2	33
III	118	15	102	1	365	7	302	56	179	3	87	89	62	...	7	55	22	...	...	22
IV	225	43	178	4	760	10	642	108	289	4	121	164	93	...	21	72	31	...	1	30
V	38	11	27	...	132	5	103	24	62	1	29	32	14	...	4	10	3	...	...	3
VI	207	52	152	3	663	12	559	92	231	1	107	123	98	...	17	81	24	...	...	24
VII	75	20	52	3	250	8	202	40	100	...	54	46	38	...	4	34	15	...	...	15
VIII	5	1	3	1	25	1	22	2	9	...	4	5	2	...	...	2	1	...	1	...
IX	3	...	3	...	19	1	14	4	11	...	7	4	3	...	1	2	...	...	...	...
X	213	41	163	9	773	21	653	99	343	1	159	183	132	1	19	112	56	...	3	53
XI	26	5	21	...	105	5	88	12	47	...	22	25	9	...	1	8	4	...	...	4
XII	76	16	60	...	238	6	197	35	102	1	44	57	45	...	11	34	16	...	5	11
XIII	81	23	58	...	310	10	274	26	113	...	68	45	52	...	13	39	16	...	1	15
XIV	7	1	6	...	29	...	25	4	16	...	7	9	9	1	4	4	3	...	...	3
XV	67	22	42	3	209	13	176	20	109	...	50	59	45	...	7	38	13	...	...	13
XVI	52	21	30	1	227	6	199	22	83	...	38	45	37	...	3	34	12	...	1	11
XVII	728	258	445	25	2,545	102	2,167	276	1,107	10	562	535	474	3	80	391	151	...	8	143
XVIII	398	125	261	12	1,255	50	1,060	145	553	4	282	267	253	3	39	211	80	...	4	76
XIX	246	92	148	6	899	21	779	99	392	2	190	200	126	...	21	105	53	...	5	48
XX	29	17	12	...	79	7	58	14	56	2	39	15	22	...	6	16	3	...	...	3
TOTAL ...	*2,817*	794	1,947	76	*9,627*	295	8,152	1,180	*4,101*	30	2,017	2,054	*1,641*	8	276	1,357	*552*	...	32	520

TABLE III.

Age, Sex and Civil Condition (by divisions) – CHRISTIANS (MALE).

DIVISION.	TOTAL.				0–5.				5–10.				10–15.			
	Total.	Unmarried.	Married.	Widowed.	Total.	Unmarried.	Married.	Widowed.	Total.	Unmarried.	Married.	Widowed.	Total.	Unmarried.	Married.	Widowed.
1	2	3	4	5	6	7	8	9	10	11	12	13	14	15	16	17
I	2,392	1,359	927	106	336	336	...	...	304	304	...	..	274	270	4	...
II	573	325	211	37	73	73	...	...	63	63	...	..	53	53	.	...
III	185	109	65	11	18	18	...	...	36	36	...	...	22	22	...	...
IV	428	253	164	11	12	12	...	...	8	8	...	...	10	10	...	.
V	1,288	793	438	57	104	104	...	...	134	134	...	...	118	118	...	...
VI	1,483	1,082	362	39	122	122	...	...	110	110	...	..	105	105	...	...
VII	913	543	315	55	119	119	...	...	122	122	...	...	104	104	...	...
VIII	46	26	19	1	3	3	...	...	3	3	...	...	9	9	...	...
IX	505	302	182	21	61	61	...	...	47	47	...	...	37	37	...	...
X	425	235	173	17	55	55	...	...	55	55	...	...	42	41	1	...
XI	2,026	1,282	660	84	236	236	...	...	262	262	...	...	254	253	1	...
XII	2,384	1,471	807	106	274	274	...	...	299	299	...	...	268	268	...	...
XIII	1,979	1,176	722	81	276	276	...	...	237	237	...	..	189	187	2	...
XIV	734	505	192	37	54	54	...	...	57	57	...	...	173	173	...	...
XV	1,062	671	360	31	132	132	...	...	112	112	...	..	122	120	2	...
XVI	1,176	688	434	54	159	159	...	...	134	134	...	...	129	128	1	...
XVII ...	272	167	98	7	33	33	...	...	32	32	...	...	20	20	...	...
XVIII	298	204	85	9	31	31	...	...	47	47	...	...	39	39	...	...
XIX	1,267	763	442	62	148	148	...	...	158	158	...		150	150	.	...
XX	1,146	703	402	41	137	137	...	...	178	178	...	...	148	147	1	...
TOTAL ...	20,582	12,657	7,058	867	2,383	2,383		...	2,398	2,398	...	...	2,266	2,254	12	...

TABLE III.

Age, Sex and Civil Condition (by divisions)—CHRISTIANS (MALE)—*continued.*

DIVISION.	15—20.				20—40.				40—55.				55—70.				70 and over.			
	Total.	Unmarried.	Married.	Widowed.	Total.	Unmarried.	Married.	Widowed.	Total.	Unmarried.	Married.	Widowed.	Total.	Unmarried.	Married.	Widowed.	Total.	Unmarried.	Married.	Widowed.
	18	19	20	21	22	23	24	25	26	27	28	29	30	31	32	33	34	35	36	37
I	200	197	3	...	738	234	482	22	345	9	291	45	152	9	118	25	43		29	14
II	50	50	...	...	196	78	114	4	100	5	75	20	30	3	19	8	8	...	3	5
III	22	21	1	...	49	11	36	2	27	1	20	6	8	...	6	2	3	..	2	1
IV	37	37	...	...	279	173	105	1	66	9	49	8	14	3	10	1	2	1	...	1
V	136	136	...	...	523	274	236	13	173	18	136	19	79	7	54	18	21	2	12	7
VI	92	92	...	...	836	630	198	8	150	22	114	14	55	1	41	13	13	...	9	4
VII	91	90	1	...	268	101	159	8	137	7	109	21	50	...	35	15	22	..	11	11
VIII	8	8	...	...	11	3	8	...	10	...	10	...	2	...	1	1	...	...	...	...
IX	49	48	1	...	206	95	106	5	72	10	55	7	30	3	19	8	3	1	1	1
X	33	33	...	...	136	46	89	1	72	5	62	5	24	...	17	7	8	...	4	4
XI	221	219	2	...	628	284	328	16	254	22	207	25	145	6	107	32	26	...	15	11
XII	285	285	...	...	731	318	399	14	327	16	269	42	156	8	116	32	44	3	23	18
XIII	176	173	3	...	649	271	365	13	297	20	252	25	117	9	81	27	38	3	19	16
XIV	76	76	...	...	223	113	104	6	101	21	68	12	42	10	16	16	8	1	4	3
XV	86	84	2	...	382	199	176	7	159	20	129	10	60	4	46	10	9	...	5	4
XVI	94	91	2	1	373	158	205	10	197	13	164	20	71	5	49	17	19	...	13	6
XVII	20	18	2	...	117	59	56	2	40	5	31	4	9	...	9	...	1	...	...	1
XVIII	30	29	1	...	101	54	45	2	32	3	26	3	13	1	11	1	5	...	2	3
XIX	118	118	...	...	422	167	245	10	177	16	138	28	77	5	53	19	17	1	11	5
XX	97	97	...	...	325	125	193	7	185	14	158	13	60	5	41	14	16	...	9	7
TOTAL ...	*1,921*	1,902	18	1	*7,193*	3,393	3,649	151	*2,921*	236	2,358	327	*1,194*	79	849	266	*306*	12	172	122

3

TABLE III.

Age, Sex and Civil Condition (by divisions)—CHRISTIANS (FEMALE).

DIVISION.	TOTAL.				0—5.				5—10.				10—15.			
	Total.	Unmarried.	Married.	Widowed.	Total.	Unmarried.	Married.	Widowed.	Total.	Unmarried.	Married.	Widowed.	Total.	Unmarried.	Married.	Widowed.
1	2	3	4	5	6	7	8	9	10	11	12	13	14	15	16	17
I	2,879	1,402	1,021	456	305	305	...	...	332	332	..	...	355	345	9	1
II	578	258	220	100	65	65	...	...	54	54	...	...	65	62	3	...
III	142	58	62	22	17	17	...	...	13	13	...	...	21	20	1	...
IV	112	53	48	11	13	13	...	...	11	11	...	...	9	9	...	...
V	1,384	743	438	203	108	108	...	...	152	152	...	...	190	185	5	...
VI	938	463	339	136	117	117	...	...	118	118	...	...	91	88	3	...
VII	978	485	345	148	118	118	...	...	111	111	...	...	107	105	2	...
VIII	44	18	16	10	6	6	...	...	5	5	...	...	4	4	...	...
IX	457	249	146	62	51	51	...	...	42	42	...	...	34	34	...	...
X	390	172	164	54	59	59	...	...	54	54	...	...	30	28	2	...
XI	2,150	1,107	721	322	248	248	...	...	263	263	...	..	242	237	5	...
XII	2,760	1,571	829	360	266	266	...	...	337	337	...	...	370	365	5	...
XIII	2,197	983	828	386	250	250	...	...	248	248	...	...	211	204	7	...
XIV	638	359	174	105	53	53	...	...	76	76	...	...	102	100	2	...
XV	1,079	546	385	148	124	124	...	...	124	124	...	...	126	125	...	1
XVI	1,180	594	427	159	160	160	...	...	145	145	...	...	123	120	3	...
XVII	211	92	85	34	24	24	...	...	22	22	...	...	16	15	1	...
XVIII	274	128	103	43	31	31	...	...	32	32	...	...	32	32	...	...
XIX	1,539	859	464	216	159	159	...	...	180	180	...	...	205	205	...	...
XX	1,300	688	403	209	143	143	...	...	170	170	...	...	143	139	4	...
TOTAL ...	*21,230*	*10,828*	*7,218*	*3,184*	*2,317*	2,317	...	...	*2,489*	2,489	...	...	*2,476*	2,422	52	2

TABLE III.

Age, Sex and Civil Condition (by divisions)—CHRISTIANS (FEMALE)—*continued.*

DIVISION.	15—20.				20—40.				40—55.				55—70.				70 and over.			
	Total.	Unmarried.	Married.	Widowed.	Total.	Unmarried.	Married.	Widowed.	Total.	Unmarried.	Married.	Widowed.	Total.	Unmarried.	Married.	Widowed.	Total.	Unmarried.	Married.	Widowed.
	18	19	20	21	22	23	24	25	26	27	28	29	30	31	32	33	34	35	36	37
I	376	237	134	5	904	151	645	108	371	27	193	151	185	4	39	142	51	1	1	49
II	60	39	21	...	213	30	152	31	113	8	38	67	8	...	6	2		...	...	...
III	18	4	13	1	50	4	40	6	16	...	6	10	6	..	2	4	1	...	...	1
IV	4	4		...	51	14	34	3	20	2	13	5	2	...	1	1	2	...	...	2
V	183	127	56	...	434	130	263	41	201	23	95	83	88	15	15	58	28	3	4	21
VI	90	56	32	2	334	72	225	37	127	9	73	45	43	3	6	34	18	...	...	18
VII	116	82	33	1	339	62	241	36	121	5	54	62	55	2	12	41	11	...	3	8
VIII	1	...	1	...	13	3	8	2	13	...	6	7	2	...	1	1	...	...	...	...
IX	51	42	8	1	199	71	111	17	59	8	21	30	21	1	6	14	...	...	...	...
X	34	17	15	2	142	10	114	18	52	3	32	17	16	1	1	14	3	...	...	3
XI	242	174	67	1	689	148	466	75	301	28	152	121	132	7	30	95	33	2	1	30
XII	308	272	34	2	972	280	597	95	304	37	156	111	157	8	35	114	46	6	2	38
XIII	226	135	90	1	755	119	555	81	317	19	147	151	150	8	27	115	40	...	2	38
XVI	73	66	6	1	209	50	123	36	90	14	36	40	21	...	7	14	14	...	...	14
XV	117	76	41	...	386	84	260	42	135	8	70	57	47	1	14	32	20	4	...	16
XVI	141	96	44	1	387	64	278	45	153	4	88	61	53	4	14	35	18	1	...	17
XVII	19	12	7	...	81	16	59	6	27	3	15	9	17	...	3	14	5	...	...	5
XVIII	28	17	11	...	98	13	74	11	38	2	15	21	13	1	2	10	2		1	1
XIX	225	156	65	4	490	136	305	49	182	14	80	88	74	5	14	55	24	4	...	20
XX	161	112	49	...	404	98	260	46	177	16	82	79	76	9	7	60	26	1	1	24
TOTAL ...	*2,473*	1,724	727	22	*7,150*	1,555	4,810	785	*2,817*	230	1,372	1,215	*1,166*	69	242	855	*342*	22	15	305

TABLE IV.

Age distribution of 1,000 MALES at certain age periods by religions and divisions (1911).

DIVISION.	HINDU.						MUSALMAN.						CHRISTIAN.					
	0—5.	5—10.	10—15.	15—20.	20—45	45 and over.	0—5.	5—10.	10—15.	15—20.	20—45.	45 and over.	0—5.	5—10.	10—15.	15—20.	20—45.	45 and over.
1	2	3	4	5	6	7	8	9	10	11.	12	13	14	15	16	17	18	19
I	128	125	102	76	400	169	94	137	114	73	378	204	140	127	115	84	362	172
II	119	101	94	80	438	168	109	119	96	83	412	181	127	110	93	87	417	166
III	116	103	103	85	430	163	106	111	124	93	370	196	97	195	119	119	319	151
IV	76	67	71	109	541	136	86	91	89	92	478	164	28	19	23	86	713	131
V	86	84	104	102	480	144	66	59	79	130	522	144	81	104	92	105	460	158
VI	83	93	95	93	484	152	82	99	110	117	454	138	82	74	71	62	608	103
VII	94	101	103	94	445	163	113	108	103	85	416	175	130	134	114	100	350	172
VIII	83	91	103	97	469	157	28	28	59	161	588	136	65	65	196	174	370	130
IX	86	88	98	98	462	170	36	23	54	63	661	163	121	93	73	97	481	135
X	122	118	112	89	396	163	108	128	135	99	344	186	129	129	99	78	388	177
XI	109	110	111	99	402	169	119	84	81	87	432	197	117	129	125	109	360	160
XII	111	116	110	99	413	151	89	89	95	116	452	159	115	125	112	120	359	169
XIII	106	112	91	85	451	155	94	98	94	79	457	178	139	120	96	89	390	166
XIV	126	111	90	79	416	178	76	71	66	33	464	290	74	77	236	103	353	157
XV	125	126	107	87	385	170	99	134	130	94	360	183	124	106	115	81	430	144
XVI	115	118	108	93	411	155	134	106	106	104	355	195	135	114	110	80	400	161
XVII	107	113	98	104	425	153	104	122	118	90	382	184	121	118	74	73	471	143
XVIII	105	106	105	101	424	159	106	131	130	94	356	183	104	158	131	101	382	124
XIX	118	120	107	86	407	162	113	130	109	93	378	177	117	125	118	93	383	164
XX	117	112	110	100	404	157	60	102	126	99	412	201	120	155	129	85	350	161
TOTAL ..	106	106	103	93	432	160	100	113	111	95	404	177	116	117	110	93	407	157

TABLE IV.

Age distribution of 1,000 FEMALES at certain age periods by religions and divisions (1911).

DIVISION.	HINDU.					MUSALMAN.					CHRISTIAN.				
	0—5.	5—10.	10—15.	15—35.	35 and over	0—5.	5—10.	10—15.	15—35.	35 and over	0—5.	5—10.	10—15.	15—35.	35 and over
1	2	3	4	5	6	7	8	9	10	11	12	13	14	15	16
I	137	125	87	380	271	74	95	67	423	341	106	115	123	385	271
II	117	111	84	411	277	107	123	104	402	264	113	93	112	419	263
III	119	109	94	390	288	104	122	109	385	280	120	91	148	423	218
IV	96	91	86	423	304	107	108	100	422	263	116	98	80	375	331
V	100	97	97	417	289	107	84	109	430	270	78	110	137	387	288
VI	92	96	93	417	302	107	112	100	425	256	125	126	97	385	267
VII	98	104	102	403	293	93	93	84	446	284	121	113	109	391	266
VIII	90	96	92	412	310	169	139	46	431	215	136	114	91	295	364
IX	103	98	96	404	299	109	109	127	400	255	112	92	74	486	236
X	136	132	93	378	261	123	135	120	359	263	151	139	77	374	259
XI	120	121	101	379	279	131	117	111	379	262	115	122	113	373	277
XII	128	122	101	379	270	118	115	98	397	272	97	122	134	394	253
XIII	129	128	100	378	265	128	133	98	375	266	114	113	96	381	296
XIV	136	115	89	373	287	92	138	35	379	356	83	119	160	348	290
XV	128	129	106	349	288	116	107	135	357	285	115	115	117	397	256
XVI	127	123	99	372	279	99	128	105	390	278	136	123	104	385	252
XVII	116	118	99	379	288	100	120	113	378	289	114	104	76	384	322
XVIII	109	113	99	378	301	107	125	109	378	281	113	117	117	376	277
XIX	124	123	105	375	273	117	127	108	381	267	103	117	133	406	241
X	126	122	100	376	276	107	90	125	348	330	110	131	110	372	277
TOTAL ...	116	114	97	389	284	107	120	108	388	277	109	117	117	388	269

TABLE V.

Education—ALL RELIGIONS.

RELIGION.	AGE.	POPULATION.									LITERATE IN ENGLISH.		
		TOTAL.			LITERATE.			ILLITERATE.					
		Persons.	Males.	Females.	Persons.	Males.	Females.	Persons.	Males.	Females.	Persons.	Males.	Females.
1	2	3	4	5	6	7	8	9	10	11	12	13	14
All religions ...	0–10	114,661	56,886	57,775	5,460	3,400	2,060	109,201	53,486	55,715	1,234	798	436
	10–15	52,816	27,709	25,107	15,925	10,625	5,300	36,891	17,084	19,807	5,511	4,225	1,286
	15–20	50,867	24,935	25,932	19,759	13,752	6,007	31,108	11,183	19,925	8,528	7,035	1,493
	20 and over ...	300,316	156,935	143,381	103,613	84,480	19,133	196,703	72,455	124,248	41,422	35,985	5,437
	GRAND TOTAL .	*518,660*	266,465	252,195	*144,757*	112,257	32,500	*373,903*	154,208	219,695	*56,695*	48,043	8,652

TABLE V.

Education--HINDUS (MALE).

DIVISION.	TOTAL OF ALL AGES.			0—10.			10—15.			15—20.			20 and over.		
	Illiterate.	Literate.	Literate in English.	Illiterate.	Literate.	Literate in English.	Illiterate.	Literate.	Literate in English.	Illiterate.	Literate.	Literate in English.	Illiterate	Literate.	Literate in English.
1	2	3	4	5	6	7	8	9	10	11	12	13	14	15	16
I	5,732	1,129	267	1,706	27	2	611	90	19	413	108	36	3,002	904	210
II	13,291	4,891	1,369	3,876	124	17	1,296	419	116	942	508	206	7,177	3,840	1,030
III	4,651	1,861	542	1,378	46	5	496	177	62	136	417	81	2,641	1,221	394
IV	2,646	2,701	1,358	708	56	9	207	172	71	202	332	246	1,529	2,091	1,032
V	3,773	4,425	2,162	1,269	122	30	406	451	214	276	559	352	1,822	3,293	1,566
VI	4,277	3,963	1,615	1,362	95	12	458	323	134	307	456	245	2,150	3,089	1,224
VII	7,357	9,407	4,801	2,974	295	50	789	932	347	497	1,082	654	3,097	7,098	3,750
VIII	6,698	7,444	2,939	2,292	165	17	807	650	211	498	879	444	3,101	5,750	2,267
IX	5,137	5,288	1,506	1,743	72	9	650	369	110	413	589	225	2,331	4,258	1,162
X	7,472	2,510	593	2,283	109	12	936	186	48	551	341	84	3,702	1,874	449
XI	11,647	7,098	2,255	3,887	223	33	1,364	724	219	1,005	847	320	5,391	5,304	1,683
XII	6,622	4,944	1,740	2,475	151	15	726	548	144	521	623	239	2,900	3,622	1,342
XIII	5,755	3,485	1,496	1,864	150	22	514	325	155	384	400	224	2,993	2,610	1,095
XIV	4,132	1,163	303	1,190	62	11	338	141	25	292	125	40	2,312	835	227
XV	3,893	1,931	656	1,406	58	3	436	187	33	262	241	107	1,789	1,445	513
XVI	6,487	5,198	2,143	2,563	162	43	732	527	229	461	622	289	2,731	3,887	1,582
XVII	6,404	5,523	2,711	2,454	164	34	697	478	211	474	771	501	2,779	4,110	1,965
XVIII	6,558	6,204	3,342	2,558	138	25	703	631	300	460	827	562	2,837	4,608	2,455
XIX	8,801	4,159	1,386	2,963	118	11	973	416	106	621	498	209	4,244	3,127	1,060
XX	5,768	3,306	1,408	1,942	133	23	615	384	173	458	449	264	2,758	2,340	948
TOTAL ..	*127,101*	*86,630*	*34,592*	42,893	2,470	383	13,754	8,130	2,927	9,173	10,724	5,328	61,281	65,306	25,954

TABLE V.

Education—HINDUS (FEMALE).

DIVISION.	TOTAL OF ALL AGES.			0—10.			10—15.			15—20.			20 and over.		
	Illiterate.	Literate.	Literate in English.	Illiterate.	Literate.	Literate in English.	Illiterate.	Literate.	Literate in English.	Illiterate.	Literate.	Literate in English.	Illiterate.	Literate.	Literate in English.
1	2	3	4	5	6	7	8	9	10	11	12	13	14	15	16
I	6,911	204	15	1,842	17	...	584	38	2	615	33	4	3,870	116	9
II	17,410	684	32	4,068	54	1	1,397	120	8	1,738	129	3	10,207	381	20
III	5,721	269	12	1,357	11	...	514	49	1	568	58	4	3,282	151	7
IV	3,327	525	38	683	40	1	238	92	10	317	123	14	2,089	270	13
V	6,197	1,082	84	1,311	126	4	551	156	18	597	216	8	3,738	584	54
VI	6,751	960	56	1,399	54	4	565	152	14	637	181	11	4,150	573	27
VII	13,728	3,277	122	3,223	207	5	1,224	516	25	1,169	597	26	8,112	1,957	66
VIII	11,269	2,214	68	2,436	80	2	902	344	17	1,014	413	19	6,917	1,377	30
IX	8,515	694	28	1,820	29	1	770	114	3	840	116	8	5,085	435	16
X	8,735	264	9	2,392	26	2	788	44	2	815	48	3	4,740	146	2
XI	16,480	1,413	75	4,205	116	6	1,532	277	11	1,539	275	20	9,204	745	38
XII	10,030	1,033	113	2,683	77	11	906	215	26	970	208	26	5,471	533	50
XIII	7,270	889	110	2,017	83	7	662	155	33	678	168	24	3,913	483	46
XIV	4,644	166	19	1,195	16	...	399	28	2	318	32	6	2,732	90	11
XV	5,420	345	14	1,457	23	...	540	70	2	479	73	2	2,944	179	10
XVI	10,185	1,153	40	2,748	85	...	910	209	11	908	231	10	5,619	628	19
XVII	10,103	1,185	71	2,558	87	2	908	217	15	923	246	20	5,719	635	34
XVIII	10,288	1,688	36	2,577	72	...	884	305	6	877	365	8	5,950	946	22
XIX	12,256	790	58	3,178	47	1	1,222	143	11	1,058	150	14	6,798	450	27
XX	7,258	846	94	1,951	61	4	658	150	17	671	183	27	3,978	452	46
TOTAL ...	*182,498*	*19,681*	*1,089*	45,100	1,811	51	16,149	3,394	234	16,731	3,845	257	104,518	11,131	547

TABLE V.

Education—MUSALMANS (MALE).

DIVISION.	TOTAL OF ALL AGES.			0—10.			10—15.			15—20.			20 and over.		
	Illiterate.	Literate.	Literate in English.	Illiterate.	Literate.	Literate in English.	Illiterate.	Literate.	Literate in English.	Illiterate.	Literate.	Literate in English.	Illiterate.	Literate.	Literate in English.
1	2	3	4	5	6	7	8	9	10	11	12	13	14	15	16
I	362	128	23	110	8	...	47	9	4	22	14	7	183	102	12
II	1,059	574	107	361	12	...	123	33	9	95	41	13	480	488	85
III	650	422	96	223	10	...	111	22	10	58	41	10	258	349	76
IV	1,610	1,121	246	461	21	...	172	72	15	128	125	37	849	903	194
V	256	353	102	66	10	4	27	21	8	38	41	15	125	281	75
VI	1,305	986	247	391	23	3	174	79	27	121	146	44	619	738	173
VII	522	180	48	153	2	...	64	8	2	40	20	6	265	150	40
VIII	98	225	22	18	...	...	13	6	...	7	45	5	60	174	17
IX	79	142	22	12	1	...	8	4	...	4	10	3	55	127	19
X	1,668	1,035	225	602	37	2	270	95	23	138	130	26	658	773	174
XI	208	142	37	70	..	...	24	4	2	10	20	6	99	118	29
XII	497	588	90	184	10	...	60	43	4	48	78	11	205	457	75
XIII	659	501	107	210	13	1	67	42	16	42	49	21	340	397	69
XIV	146	37	10	26	1	...	8	4	3	4	2	2	108	30	5
XV	447	247	93	158	4	...	67	23	5	35	30	25	187	190	63
XVI	409	299	107	167	3	1	51	24	3	42	32	17	149	240	86
XVII	4,853	2,582	906	1,573	112	22	627	246	78	358	310	154	2,295	1,914	652
XVIII	2,381	1,255	362	842	21	3	354	118	47	216	126	52	969	990	260
XIX	1,883	747	181	611	27	3	226	61	20	162	84	24	884	575	134
XX	228	110	25	60	4	...	35	7	3	24	9	4	114	90	18
TOTAL ...	*19,310*	*11,674*	*3,056*	6,288	314	39	2,528	921	279	1,592	1,353	482	8,902	9,086	2,256

TABLE V.

Education—MUSALMANS (FEMALE).

DIVISION.	TOTAL OF ALL AGES.			0—10.			10—15.			15—20.			20 and over.		
	Illiterate.	Literate.	Literate in English.	Illiterate.	Literate.	Literate in English.	Illiterate.	Literate.	Literate in English.	Illiterate.	Literate.	Literate in English.	Illiterate.	Literate.	Literate in English.
1	2	3	4	5	6	7	8	9	10	11	12	13	14	15	16
I	510	15	...	88	1	...	35	...	...	54	2	...	333	12	...
II	1,501	62	...	358	2	...	154	8	...	160	7	..	829	45	...
III	1,066	55	...	251	2	...	115	7	...	111	7	...	589	39	...
IV	1,866	174	8	431	8	...	175	28	2	192	33	1	1,068	105	5
V	304	53	...	68	...	...	28	11	...	24	14	...	184	27	...
VI	1,651	145	6	385	8	...	155	25	2	181	26	...	930	66	4
VII	626	29	...	121	1	...	53	2	...	65	10	...	387	16	...
VIII	63	2	...	20	...	...	3	...	...	4	1	...	36	1	...
IX	51	4	...	10	2	...	6	1	...	3	...	...	32	1	...
X	2,248	188	3	621	6	...	261	31	1	180	33	1	1,186	118	1
XI	273	25	...	72	2	...	26	7	...	24	2	...	151	14	...
XII	662	51	...	162	4	...	66	4	...	65	11	...	369	32	...
XIII	833	60	11	230	3	1	80	8	...	64	17	8	459	32	2
XIV	84	3	...	20	...	...	1	2	...	7	...	...	56	1	...
XV	616	74	2	151	3	...	79	14	...	51	16	1	335	41	1
XVI	554	62	2	140	...	...	53	12	...	44	8	...	317	42	2
XVII	6,911	588	29	1,621	30	2	756	87	8	626	102	3	3,908	369	16
XVIII	3,493	361	6	879	16	...	360	60	...	334	64	...	1,920	221	6
XIX	2,488	161	5	637	6	...	267	18	1	223	23	1	1,356	114	3
XX	255	24	2	52	3	...	32	3	...	24	5	...	147	13	2
TOTAL ...	26,050	2,135	74	6,317	97	3	2,705	328	14	2,436	381	15	14,592	1,329	42

TABLE V.

Education—CHRISTIANS (MALE).

DIVISION.	TOTAL OF ALL AGES.			0—10.			10—15.			15—20.			20 and over.		
	Illiterate.	Literate.	Literate in English.	Illiterate.	Literate.	Literate in English.	Illiterate.	Literate.	Literate in English.	Illiterate.	Literate.	Literate in English.	Illiterate.	Literate.	Literate in English.
1	2	3	4	5	6	7	8	9	10	11	12	13	14	15	16
I	1,184	1,308	840	576	64	35	135	139	80	68	132	95	405	873	630
II	274	299	218	127	9	6	23	30	26	13	37	24	111	223	162
III	108	82	47	52	2	...	11	11	3	9	13	6	31	56	38
IV	70	358	277	16	4	4	3	7	7	3	34	24	48	313	242
V	386	902	770	197	41	32	47	71	59	25	111	91	117	679	588
VI	400	1,063	953	207	25	21	41	64	50	24	68	52	128	926	830
VII	301	612	494	201	40	28	23	81	67	17	74	64	60	417	335
VIII	25	21	11	5	1	...	5	4	2	3	5	3	12	11	6
IX	144	361	302	98	10	2	4	33	27	10	39	35	32	279	238
X	174	251	183	100	10	4	22	20	14	7	26	17	45	195	148
XI	760	1,266	960	433	65	40	83	171	100	45	176	140	199	854	680
XII	806	1,578	1,218	496	77	63	81	187	125	41	244	197	188	1,070	833
XIII	743	1,236	966	445	68	35	63	126	87	37	139	105	198	903	739
XIV	157	577	482	79	32	25	9	164	133	7	69	66	62	312	258
XV	347	715	588	225	19	10	43	79	24	9	77	52	70	540	442
XVI	448	728	568	252	41	22	52	77	53	18	76	63	126	534	430
XVII	95	177	156	61	4	3	11	9	6	2	18	15	21	146	132
XVIII	97	201	163	64	14	6	13	26	19	4	26	23	16	135	115
XIX	485	782	574	275	31	12	47	103	69	22	96	76	141	552	417
XX	538	608	433	275	40	24	65	83	45	27	70	48	171	415	316
TOTAL ...	*7,537*	*13,045*	*10,143*	4,184	597	372	781	1,485	996	391	1,530	1,196	2,181	9,433	7,579

TABLE V.

Education—CHRISTIANS (FEMALE).

DIVISION.	TOTAL OF ALL AGES.			0—10.			10—15.			15—20.			20 and over.		
	Illiterate.	Literate.	Literate in English.	Illiterate.	Literate.	Literate in English.	Illiterate.	Literate.	Literate in English.	Illiterate.	Literate.	Literate in English.	Illiterate.	Literate.	Literate in English.
1	2	3	4	5	6	7	8	9	10	11	12	13	14	15	16
I	1,707	1,172	708	568	69	42	160	195	133	132	244	155	847	664	378
II	379	199	132	110	9	6	48	22	17	32	28	13	194	140	96
III	108	34	14	28	2	...	16	5	1	10	8	3	54	19	10
IV	37	75	66	19	5	5	3	6	6	...	4	3	15	60	52
V	535	849	687	190	61	55	47	143	115	38	145	123	251	500	394
VI	540	398	278	216	19	14	47	44	27	30	60	33	247	275	204
VII	445	538	379	191	38	20	42	65	41	30	86	65	182	344	253
VIII	28	16	6	10	1	...	2	2	1	...	1	...	16	12	5
IX	159	298	279	79	14	14	13	31	20	11	40	37	56	223	208
X	246	144	108	108	5	3	24	6	3	17	17	10	97	116	92
XI	976	1,174	784	452	59	24	82	160	106	58	184	120	384	771	534
XII	1,116	1,644	1,202	506	97	55	88	282	185	55	253	193	467	1,012	769
XIII	1,145	1,052	708	441	57	34	92	119	77	77	149	89	535	727	508
XIV	216	422	337	72	57	32	12	90	69	10	63	47	122	212	189
XV	589	490	314	225	23	4	56	70	25	33	84	49	275	313	236
XVI	647	533	415	272	33	21	46	77	53	44	97	72	285	326	269
XVII	93	119	109	35	11	8	9	7	7	8	11	11	40	90	83
XVIII	160	114	91	61	2	1	18	14	11	7	21	20	74	77	59
XIX	794	745	479	298	41	16	56	149	84	61	164	107	379	391	272
XX	795	505	328	276	37	24	71	72	43	68	93	57	380	303	204
TOTAL ...	*10,714*	*10,516*	*7,424*	4,166	640	378	927	1,549	1,024	721	1,752	1,207	4,900	6,575	4,815

TABLE

BIRTH

DISTRICTS, ETC.	TOTAL POPULATION. Total.	Males.	Females.	I. Males.	I. Females.	II. Males.	II. Females.	III. Males.	III. Females.
1	2	3	4	5	6	7	8	9	10
A.—MADRAS PRESIDENCY.									
I.—British Districts.									
Ganjám	793	477	316	3	9	12	15	16	14
Vizagapatam	1,397	758	639	51	38	41	52	25	18
Gódávari	957	583	374	26	21	17	16	18	9
Kistna	1,377	804	573	20	...	83	31	24	18
Guntúr	1,300	785	515	6	16	86	24	20	12
Nellore	7,594	4,424	3,170	45	52	321	304	416	170
Cuddapah	1,079	613	466	14	8	21	11	9	12
Kurnool	395	228	167	4	13	8	2	7	5
Bellary	1,421	757	664	18	19	22	19	35	41
Anantapur	224	144	80	...	4	2	..	1	...
Madras	345,317	172,729	172,588	8,118	8,571	13,163	13,254	4,721	4,554
Chingleput	69,576	34,447	35,129	542	770	3,713	3,842	1,545	1,552
North Arcot	23,667	12,526	11,141	169	164	914	888	325	313
Chittoor	737	454	283	...	...	21	21	...	...
Salem	3,314	1,869	1,445	33	35	69	69	26	24
Coimbatore	2,134	1,241	893	25	26	33	19	15	13
South Arcot	9,859	5,049	4,810	171	168	525	518	130	113
Tanjore	9,496	5,352	4,144	69	78	118	116	62	49
Trichinopoly	4,312	2,391	1,921	36	71	156	124	68	62
Madura	3,253	1,897	1,356	34	40	152	188	8	7
Ramnad	168	119	49	...	...	6	...	...	...
Tinnevelly	3,790	2,174	1,616	30	52	329	304	16	15
Nilgiris	600	338	262	8	8	9	8	1	1
Malabar	2,911	2,093	818	20	38	58	12	23	25
South Canara	873	605	268	4	8	36	29	15	5
Anjengo	31	12	19	...	...	1	1	...	...
TOTAL ...	*496,575*	*252,869*	*243,706*	9,446	10,209	19,866	19,867	7,526	7,033
II.—Feudatory States.	1,312	901	411	10	16	42	17	6	3
TOTAL ...	*497,887*	*253,770*	*244,117*	9,456	10,225	19,908	19,884	7,532	7,036
B.—OTHER PROVINCES AND STATES IN INDIA.									
Mysore State	5,341	2,924	2,417	57	50	108	83	73	61
Bombay Presidency (including Feudatory States)	2,614	1,623	991	49	59	76	74	57	53
Hyderabad State	2,318	1,448	870	12	19	65	34	61	64
Other Provinces and States	5,318	3,522	1,796	77	64	76	47	75	56
Foreign Possessions in India	2,189	1,084	1,105	70	73	141	105	18	25
TOTAL ...	*17,780*	*10,601*	*7,179*	265	265	466	343	284	259
C.—OTHER ASIATIC COUNTRIES ...	582	359	223	11	25	12	1	4	4
D.—EUROPE.									
United Kingdom ...	2,003	1,472	531	32	28	8	4	...	1
Other European Countries	244	161	83	1	4	...	4	...	...
TOTAL ...	*2,247*	*1,633*	*614*	33	32	8	8	..	1
E.—OTHERS ...	164	102	62	3	3	2	3	...	...
GRAND TOTAL ...	*518,660*	*266,465*	*252,195*	*9,768*	*10,550*	*20,396*	*20,239*	*7,820*	*7,300*

VI.

PLACE.

IV.		V.		VI.		VII.		VIII.		IX.	
Males.	Females.	Males.	Females.	Males.	Females.	Males.	Females.	Males.	Females.	Males.	Females.
11	12	13	14	15	16	17	18	19	20	21	22
15	4	40	20	3	5	10	5	13	2	7	6
13	...	46	35	9	15	17	35	20	17	10	6
38	3	25	13	29	24	34	29	33	24	10	8
61	5	68	30	65	53	54	48	63	57	22	13
44	3	37	17	110	90	108	75	146	108	26	20
131	61	97	76	344	290	338	335	703	511	135	130
12	13	12	9	58	37	42	45	105	38	48	41
7	2	14	4	15	6	20	15	17	12	7	6
13	5	28	19	51	32	48	58	34	30	39	15
4	1	3	1	27	15	10	4	28	13	6	4
4,698	4,501	5,352	5,596	7,274	7,181	12,716	13,096	8,454	8,569	6,260	6,199
592	572	1,297	1,246	1,184	1,144	2,712	2,807	1,845	1,917	1,509	1,324
184	188	796	574	656	449	909	870	963	840	838	659
5	4	10	1	9	6	1	1	31	23	20	5
76	44	78	71	106	43	94	79	228	160	115	55
88	34	83	49	37	21	49	55	77	47	51	22
181	63	224	196	164	153	220	236	234	202	185	148
429	118	430	318	209	165	290	243	281	179	258	193
127	56	177	138	46	72	101	101	151	87	110	49
347	47	183	69	45	31	51	27	61	56	228	162
14	...	37	1	3	2	...	...	11	5	3	1
194	19	158	99	65	27	27	39	230	248	58	14
14	2	13	7	16	13	11	9	6	4	13	16
221	27	211	59	51	28	29	20	81	22	80	33
23	3	45	14	28	3	7	6	7	1	64	19
2	...	...	...	...	...	..	1	...	...	4	2
7,528	5,775	9,464	8,662	10,604	9,905	17,898	18,239	13,822	13,172	10,106	9,150
116	14	102	31	17	19	9	15	8	13	20	15
7,644	5,789	9,566	8,693	10,621	9,924	17,907	18,254	13,830	13,185	10,126	9,165
60	33	118	125	170	149	174	164	161	130	116	91
115	38	138	69	186	105	69	62	152	74	356	198
40	10	36	29	262	73	53	34	88	33	60	46
393	58	145	43	131	64	140	98	616	226	406	137
64	39	53	42	82	74	46	35	45	48	41	29
672	173	490	308	831	465	482	398	1,057	511	979	501
55	5	32	11	16	16	13	3	...	...	21	12
122	30	32	29	539	29	4	1	...	...	71	41
62	6	11	5	10	3	1	3	...	...	6	5
184	36	43	34	549	32	5	4	...	...	77	46
2	4	1	1	10	9	3	1	...	2	7	8
8,557	*6,007*	*10,132*	*9,047*	*12,027*	*10,446*	*18,410*	*18,655*	*14,887*	*13,698*	*11,210*	*9,727*

TABLE

BIRTH PLACE

DISTRICTS, ETC.	X.		XI.		XII.		XIII.		XIV.	
	Males.	Females.	Males.	Females.	Males.	Females.	Males.	Females.	Males.	Females.
	23	24	25	26	27	28	29	30	31	32
A.—MADRAS PRESIDENCY.										
I.—British Districts.										
Ganjám	183	159	17	29	17	13	26	5	15	2
Vizagapatam	155	154	46	53	28	40	31	29	16	15
Gódávari	39	40	20	23	19	10	36	22	22	9
Kistna	31	20	29	31	31	42	26	17	3	7
Guntúr	14	12	35	21	34	30	31	16	10	9
Nellore	160	78	576	258	74	104	188	124	67	61
Cuddapah	39	30	21	33	22	37	18	20	22	9
Kurnool	6	20	13	15	9	4	23	3	7	3
Bellary	75	65	38	49	84	71	48	40	14	11
Anantapur	.	...	8	7	8	4	7	5	2	1
Madras	7,901	7,324	13,845	13,592	8,956	9,240	7,906	7,688	3,960	3,752
Chingleput	2,229	2,142	3,318	3,372	1,994	2,033	1,328	1,281	1,068	1,020
North Arcot	610	775	878	743	1,212	988	608	479	281	211
Chittoor	134	...	122	139	10	5	19	12	1	2
Salem	58	54	64	77	197	90	69	65	32	18
Coimbatore	23	13	46	55	86	73	94	41	26	17
South Arcot	189	113	408	386	386	376	272	304	99	80
Tanjore	69	43	242	230	320	313	271	233	79	33
Trichinopoly	139	106	181	166	154	110	146	140	33	12
Madura	20	20	289	251	58	88	102	46	20	10
Ramnad	...	...	2	3	1	...	2	4	2	1
Tinnevelly	32	19	108	101	75	169	229	98	26	16
Nilgiris	13	14	21	23	40	...	28	27	23	12
Malabar	48	48	83	44	221	87	208	93	60	20
South Canara	13	12	15	11	88	62	49	12	10	5
Anjengo	:	...	...	...	...	...	...	...	...	1
TOTAL ..	**12,181**	**11,261**	**20,425**	**19,712**	**14,124**	**13,989**	**11,764**	**10,804**	**5,898**	**5,337**
II.—Feudatory States.	25	32	51	30	179	35	53	33	7	6
TOTAL ...	**12,206**	**11,293**	**20,476**	**19,742**	**14,303**	**14,024**	**11,817**	**10,837**	**5,905**	**5,343**
B.—OTHER PROVINCES AND STATES IN INDIA.										
Mysore State	246	145	203	200	265	156	195	159	59	60
Bombay Presidency (including Feudatory States)	51	35	70	38	73	35	27	30	17	13
Hyderabad State ...	300	152	88	78	78	34	54	46	29	7
Other Provinces and States	258	163	170	180	283	177	136	74	6	30
Foreign Possessions in India	28	30	94	100	44	76	60	69	14	17
TOTAL ...	**883**	**525**	**625**	**596**	**743**	**478**	**472**	**378**	**188**	**127**
C.—OTHER ASIATIC COUNTRIES ...	9	7	26	15	22	17	33	13	7	10
D.—EUROPE.										
United Kingdom ...	33	15	21	10	65	80	97	46	104	49
Other European Countries	1	1	5	...	6	4	8	7	10	3
TOTAL ...	**34**	**16**	**26**	**10**	**71**	**84**	**105**	**53**	**114**	**52**
E.—OTHERS ...	5	1	4	3	33	1	3	6	2	3
GRAND TOTAL ...	***13,137***	***11,842***	***21,157***	***20,366***	***15,172***	***14,604***	***12,430***	***11,287***	***6,216***	***5,535***

VI.

—continued.

XV.		XVI.		XVII.		XVIII.		XIX.		XX.	
Males.	Females.	Males.	Females.	Males.	Females.	Males.	Females.	Males.	Females.	Males.	Females.
33	34	35	36	37	38	39	40	41	42	43	44
11	5	11	1	22	10	32	10	21	2	3	...
71	22	11	10	23	28	39	19	23	13	83	40
16	14	9	10	41	14	74	39	49	39	28	7
30	32	37	36	88	26	58	48	46	43	15	16
3	..	10	4	14	9	38	37	6	9	7	2
55	36	84	65	187	114	138	59	274	246	91	96
6	7	19	11	57	52	57	28	23	22	8	3
9	6	9	16	26	8	14	12	9	11	4	4
29	17	48	40	43	52	51	37	21	16	18	28
..	...	3	4	14	6	11	8	5	1	5	2
5,281	5,380	9,364	9,283	14,335	14,554	10,957	11,056	12,576	12,647	6,892	6,551
895	992	1,951	1,912	1,395	1,496	1,754	1,822	2,124	2,518	1,452	1,367
232	238	602	525	953	841	740	808	404	379	252	209
17	22	27	22	1	4	10	13	6	2	10	1
28	39	93	87	133	129	166	136	67	61	137	109
34	35	35	37	113	72	201	147	47	61	83	56
186	188	311	356	308	317	360	351	330	371	166	171
59	69	194	175	505	375	694	537	185	171	588	506
34	41	100	93	220	168	259	206	51	59	103	60
23	17	17	21	74	52	91	82	45	104	49	38
7	9	7	7	7	2	4	4	5	8	8	2
43	25	43	19	90	57	246	180	110	68	65	47
31	41	19	13	20	15	9	4	80	34	13	11
41	16	113	38	191	63	144	57	97	42	113	46
3	4	24	10	71	30	47	8	32	18	24	8
1	1	1	1	...	...	2	1	...	11	...	...
7,145	**7,256**	**13,142**	**12,796**	**18,931**	**18,494**	**16,196**	**15,709**	**16,586**	**16,956**	**10,217**	**9,380**
27	13	25	23	86	19	65	24	29	18	24	35
7,172	**7,269**	**13,167**	**12,819**	**19,017**	**18,513**	**16,261**	**15,733**	**16,615**	**16,974**	**10,241**	**9,415**
94	81	149	103	218	198	243	238	114	114	101	77
14	12	31	1	78	47	31	28	14	13	19	12
19	19	47	42	74	79	42	32	29	31	16	8
98	53	80	85	152	74	66	41	96	80	55	46
23	18	46	64	38	49	50	49	48	65	79	98
248	**183**	**353**	**295**	**560**	**447**	**432**	**388**	**301**	**303**	**270**	**241**
15	15	45	27	22	20	7	...	7	13	2	9
171	74	22	7	35	20	19	6	61	41	36	20
8	9	3	2	1	2	3	...	11	23	14	2
179	**83**	**25**	**9**	**36**	**22**	**22**	**6**	**72**	**64**	**50**	**22**
8	8	11	1	1	5	2	...	3	6	2	2
7,622	***7,558***	***13,601***	***13,151***	***19,636***	***19,007***	***16,724***	***16,127***	***16,998***	***17,360***	***10,565***	***9,689***

TABLE VII.

Caste, Tribe or Race.

RELIGION AND CASTE, TRIBE, RACE OR NATIONALITY.	POPULATION.			POPULATION (BOTH SEXES) IN EACH DIVISION.																			
	Total.	Males.	Females.	I.	II.	III.	IV.	V.	VI.	VII.	VIII.	IX.	X.	XI.	XII.	XIII.	XIV.	XV.	XVI.	XVII.	XVIII.	XIX.	XX.
1	2	3	4	5	6	7	8	9	10	11	12	13	14	15	16	17	18	19	20	21	22	23	24
PART (1) HINDU.																							
(a) Tamil Castes.																							
1. AMBATTAN	2,536	1,192	1,344	29	259	75	11	116	107	274	391	21	123	170	47	209	6	90	103	154	82	165	104
2. BRÁHMAN	20,727	12,055	8,672	55	328	116	1,157	2,896	149	1,407	1,717	1,570	32	343	720	653	50	480	774	1,565	3,918	675	2,122
3. CHETTI	10,732	5,434	5,298	269	1,376	63	2,175	850	42	71	106	2,416	61	712	282	184	43	50	578	448	300	570	136
4. IDAIYAN	14,308	7,378	6,930	264	812	289	122	439	757	1,062	1,021	775	419	1,715	947	889	1	514	703	1,086	895	1,180	468
5. KAMMÁLAN	15,626	7,916	7,710	117	704	208	652	646	23	644	112	2,159	267	2,648	308	1,060	35	237	2,046	1,275	1,344	989	152
6. KANAKKAN	3,396	1,782	1,614	53	83	39	32	185	369	1,034	357	34	16	327	229	53	15	25	126	219	47	139	14
7. KURAVAN	1,382	684	698	..	17	52	4	...	1	92	254	7	371	29	...	221	48	2	3	64	...	217	...
8. PALLI	50,209	26,069	24,140	1,823	8,212	2,187	473	1,889	526	1,009	1,063	1,736	2,177	5,949	2,602	922	416	2,645	3,511	3,422	2,531	4,715	2,401
9. PANDÁRAM	1,624	851	773	11	335	16	36	101	109	68	51	48	23	373	24	76	6	16	33	43	114	105	36
10. PANJIRAVAN	1,088	498	590	...	2	4	99	50	11	341	41	...	36	138	67	79	1	15	88	62	8	34	12
11. PARAIYAN	59,651	29,589	30,062	2,089	3,020	2,789	1,514	1,530	1,947	2,977	906	1,171	4,882	3,512	5,207	4,985	3,239	4,941	4,470	2,814	964	4,116	2,578
12. PATTANAVAN	9,799	5,223	4,576	6,650	139	123	7	...	...	5	63	...	...	23	24	...	...	8	107	25	1,588	588	449
13. SEMBADAVAN	1,278	640	638	6	122	...	4	2	7	22	7	31	23	80	21	6	13	20	203	14	27	204	466
14. SHÁNÁN	7,716	3,971	3,745	130	1,967	901	8	1	35	83	23	8	151	445	263	53	134	64	71	92	217	1,888	1,182
15. VALLUVAN	2,928	2,035	893	39	241	86	163	38	106	371	30	22	812	291	54	88	362	47	40	8	27	102	1
16. VÁNIYAN	15,496	7,416	8,080	182	3,535	113	314	1,148	325	663	1,329	347	436	949	1,384	1,140	170	36	511	25	1,955	470	464
17. VANNÁN	4,210	2,660	1,550	75	1,623	66	20	27	252	15	26	17	193	66	76	101	1,181	41	1	21	22	161	26
18. VELLÁLA	66,551	32,409	34,142	778	3,279	1,295	382	1,517	3,360	12,031	5,132	1,187	2,213	7,399	4,283	1,888	695	829	5,129	4,881	3,096	4,330	2,847
19. OTHERS	3,908	2,050	1,858	111	481	66	244	73	119	110	90	79	320	609	225	141	37	49	26	85	551	329	163
TOTAL ...	*295,165*	149,852	143,313	12,681	26,735	8,488	7,417	11,508	8,245	22,279	12,719	11,628	12,555	25,778	16,763	12,748	6,452	10,109	18,523	16,303	17,686	20,927	13,621
(b) Telugu Castes.																							
20. BALIJA	47,811	23,521	24,290	367	3,796	1,225	717	1,690	3,385	6,593	6,261	1,286	2,262	5,379	3,122	1,357	309	660	2,439	2,495	2,199	1,680	589
21. BRÁHMAN	5,436	2,995	2,441	14	278	119	114	530	180	1,262	489	298	30	211	116	76	14	89	334	313	569	72	328
22. CHAKKALIYAN ...	1,184	587	597	154	79	46	19	6	19	3	1	1	2	103	281	5	12	24	...	305	12	102	10
23. DÉVÁNGA	1,901	951	950	...	706	985	20	8	6	12	113	4	2	8	2	10	5	...	...	...	11	1	8
24. JANAPPAN	2,060	957	1,103	23	344	...	...	...	2	...	172	550	...	115	331	503	...	...	...	3	...	15	2
25. KAMMA	1,872	928	944	57	86	102	18	150	155	113	123	74	50	177	233	350	1	2	5	50	116	3	7
26. KÁPU	1,919	1,136	783	27	141	98	40	67	96	98	76	71	497	137	95	158	32	13	46	17	84	87	39
27. KÓMATI...	4,144	2,172	1,972	50	60	12	30	26	879	271	2,051	308	...	13	12	14	43	8	...	65	189	61	52
28. MÁDIGA	7,048	3,701	3,347	77	643	308	2	27	27	...	634	2	2,196	666	309	846	29	209	...	143	41	865	24
29. MANGALA	1,628	827	801	29	150	63	18	39	52	18	101	304	56	207	42	8	10	30	8	107	332	15	39
30. ODDE	1,758	895	863	5	118	...	15	6	1	...	154	32	314	211	8	84	152	...	15	14	1	628	...
31. SÁLE	4,444	2,406	2,038	9	627	497	12	8	601	410	37	21	5	...	18	78	18	4	7	60	235	227	1,570
32. SÁTÁNI	1,982	896	1,086	5	380	69	1	5	49	396	54	120	68	561	45	12	14	18	24	24	88	40	9
33. UPPARA	4,221	1,969	2,232	9	13	8	6	...	...	...	2	4	189	880	2	...	2,576	...	11	...	...	363	158
34. VAISYA	6,042	3,050	2,992	36	202	81	233	457	604	243	2,046	1,452	13	150	12	28	1	3	193	96	63	92	37
35. OTHERS...	4,216	2,746	1,470	60	227	95	124	106	909	466	303	88	362	426	80	313	196	148	45	38	107	77	96
TOTAL ...	*97,666*	49,757	47,909	922	7,850	3,708	1,369	3,125	6,965	9,885	12,617	4,565	6,046	9,244	4,708	3,842	3,412	1,208	3,127	3,780	4,047	4,328	2,968

TABLE VII.

Caste, Tribe or Race—*continued.*

RELIGION AND CASTE, TRIBE, RACE OR NATIONALITY.	POPULATION.			POPULATION (BOTH SEXES) IN EACH DIVISION.																			
	Total.	Males.	Females.	I.	II.	III.	IV.	V.	VI.	VII.	VIII.	IX.	X.	XI.	XII.	XIII.	XIV.	XV.	XVI.	XVII.	XVIII.	XIX.	XX.
1	2	3	4	5	6	7	8	9	10	11	12	13	14	15	16	17	18	19	20	21	22	23	24
PART (i) HINDU—*cont.*																							
(c) **Malayálam Castes.**																							
36. Náyar	1,066	936	150	9	104	4	9	93	37	7	14	23	7	27	190	145	12	16	143	101	71	53	21
37. Others	402	334	68	6	18	5	24	24	12	11	12	8	...	22	91	64	32	4	10	23	8	21	7
TOTAL ...	*1,468*	**1,270**	**218**	**15**	**122**	**9**	**33**	**117**	**49**	**18**	**26**	**31**	**7**	**49**	**281**	**209**	**44**	**20**	**153**	**124**	**79**	**74**	**28**
(d) **Canarese Castes.**																							
38. Bráhman	2,054	1,200	854	1	92	12	101	157	15	65	51	61	3	13	77	107	4	2	40	183	890	47	133
39. Others	1,417	767	650	13	81	55	12	27	69	234	145	159	56	90	1	8	5	87	13	274	47	36	5
TOTAL ...	*3,471*	**1,967**	**1,504**	**14**	**173**	**67**	**113**	**184**	**84**	**299**	**196**	**220**	**59**	**103**	**78**	**115**	**9**	**89**	**53**	**457**	**937**	**83**	**138**
40. (e) **Oriya Castes** ...	110	86	24	2	10	...	46	14	...	...	1	...	1	14	...	13	3	...	...	...	2	4	...
(f) **Madras, other languages.**																							
41. Bráhman	4,510	2,591	1,919	24	103	82	21	132	49	102	345	1,222	26	140	191	76	17	5	45	350	1,265	78	237
42. Kshatriya	8,466	4,291	4,175	288	1,078	87	63	165	133	804	717	203	40	864	404	257	136	97	672	1,710	372	309	67
43. Mahráti	2,484	1,288	1,196	8	46	18	4	75	90	154	439	639	129	204	121	78	15	4	137	163	56	61	43
44. Rájput	1,499	892	607	8	52	26	48	84	211	61	24	82	65	108	47	23	3	27	184	287	121	74	14
45. Others	2,253	1,247	1,006	4	49	6	75	57	107	112	422	914	26	127	34	22	12	29	124	38	21	25	49
TOTAL ...	*19,212*	**10,309**	**8,903**	**332**	**1,328**	**219**	**211**	**513**	**590**	**1,233**	**1,947**	**3,010**	**286**	**1,443**	**797**	**456**	**183**	**162**	**1,162**	**2,548**	**1,835**	**547**	**410**
46. (g) **Foreign Languages.**	510	296	214	6	7	4	8	16	18	46	101	95	8	1	2	11	...	1	...	34	140	12	...
47. **Caste not stated** ..	288	194	94	4	51	7	2	...	...	9	18	85	19	6	...	5	2	...	5	19	12	31	13
TOTAL PART (i) HINDU.	*415,910*	*213,731*	*202,179*	*13,976*	*36,276*	*12,502*	*9,199*	*15,477*	*15,951*	*33,769*	*27,625*	*19,634*	*18,981*	*36,638*	*22,629*	*17,399*	*10,105*	*11,589*	*23,023*	*23,215*	*24,738*	*26,006*	*17,178*
PART (ii) MUSALMAN.																							
48. Labbai	5,073	2,895	2,178	71	518	31	622	107	122	20	38	51	88	36	234	358	26	26	120	332	1,720	470	33
49. Pathán	4,040	2,183	1,857	21	206	224	143	54	188	73	31	14	807	75	157	175	44	189	102	930	243	336	28
50. Saiyad	10,014	5,171	4,843	67	428	335	501	59	271	165	28	14	671	86	209	378	46	396	227	3,282	1,526	1,258	67
51. Sheik	38,000	19,392	18,608	829	1,983	1,565	3,148	433	3,342	1,075	233	130	3,456	409	1,115	1,074	143	739	857	10,116	3,805	3,106	442
52. Others	2,042	1,343	699	27	61	38	357	312	164	24	8	67	117	37	83	68	11	34	18	274	196	104	42
TOTAL PART (ii) MUSALMAN	*59,169*	*30,984*	*28,185*	*1,015*	*3,196*	*2,193*	*4,771*	*965*	*4,087*	*1,357*	*388*	*276*	*5,139*	*643*	*1,798*	*2,053*	*270*	*1,384*	*1,324*	*14,934*	*7,490*	*5,274*	*612*

TABLE VII.

Caste, Tribe or Race—*continued.*

Religion and Caste, Tribe, Race or Nationality.	Population.			Population (both sexes) in each Division.																			
	Total.	Males.	Females.	I.	II.	III.	IV.	V.	VI.	VII.	VIII.	IX.	X.	XI.	XII.	XIII.	XIV.	XV.	XVI.	XVII.	XVIII.	XIX.	XX.
1	2	3	4	5	6	7	8	9	10	11	12	13	14	15	16	17	18	19	20	21	22	23	24
PART (iii) CHRISTIAN.																							
53. Indian Christian ...	27,293	13,121	14,172	4,380	824	313	239	1,632	1,213	1,102	90	293	498	3,112	2,857	2,602	638	1,532	1,367	189	391	2,180	1,846
54. Anglo Indian	10,332	4,917	5,415	743	293	11	42	855	566	768	...	421	224	785	1,783	1,145	404	204	887	208	145	411	437
Foreign.																							
55. English	1,526	1,205	321	32	7	1	100	31	555	2	...	88	37	20	63	105	109	179	18	52	13	69	45
56. European (unspecified).	2,071	930	1,141	108	26	2	16	108	65	12	...	124	46	235	399	276	168	154	81	24	10	107	110
57. Others	590	409	181	8	1	...	143	46	22	7	...	36	10	24	42	48	58	72	3	10	13	39	8
TOTAL PART (iii) CHRISTIAN	*41,812*	*20,582*	*21,230*	*5,271*	*1,151*	*327*	*540*	*2,672*	*2,421*	*1,891*	*90*	*962*	*815*	*1,176*	*5,144*	*4,176*	*1,372*	*2,141*	*2,356*	*483*	*572*	*2,806*	*2,446*
PART (iv).																							
58. Jain, Buddhist, Parsi, Jew and others ...	1,769	1,168	601	56	12	98	54	65	14	48	482	65	44	66	205	89	4	66	49	11	51	272	18
GRAND TOTAL OF ALL RELIGIONS	*518,660*	*266,465*	*252,195*	*20,318*	*40,635*	*15,120*	*14,564*	*19,179*	*22,473*	*37,065*	*28,585*	*20,937*	*24,979*	*41,523*	*29,776*	*23,717*	*11,751*	*15,180*	*26,752*	*38,643*	*32,851*	*34,358*	*20,254*

TABLE VIII.

Territorial distribution of the Christian Population by Sect and Race.

SECT.	RACE.	POPULATION RETURNED.			POPULATION (BOTH SEXES) IN EACH DIVISION.																			
		Total.	Males.	Females.	I.	II.	III.	IV.	V.	VI.	VII.	VIII.	IX.	X.	XI.	XII.	XIII.	XIV.	XV.	XVI.	XVII.	XVIII.	XIX.	XX.
1	2	3	4	5	6	7	8	9	10	11	12	13	14	15	16	17	18	19	20	21	22	23.	24	25
1. ANGLICANS ...	Europeans ...	2,586	1,620	966	101	27	...	91	58	509	8	...	167	44	184	319	257	196	246	81	59	21	114	104
	Anglo Indians	4,343	2,126	2,217	333	88	6	24	179	164	156	...	239	109	465	852	453	256	141	477	99	42	104	156
	Indians ...	3,805	1,811	1,994	177	69	9	30	165	87	149	13	62	40	787	683	268	99	260	229	27	66	451	134
	TOTAL ...	*10,734*	5,557	5,177	611	184	15	145	402	760	313	13	468	193	1,436	1,854	978	551	647	787	185	129	669	394
2. BAPTISTS ...	Europeans ...	32	20	12	...	...	1	2	...	8	...	...	3	...	5	8	3	...	2	...	...	...	...	...
	Anglo Indians.	62	27	35	...	16	...	...	2	...	...	...	5	16	6	...	8	...	2	...	7	...	...	...
	Indians ...	404	190	214	15	55	22	...	3	3	13	39	5	31	82	106	9	..	9	...	...	1	10	1
	TOTAL ...	*498*	237	261	15	71	23	2	5	11	13	39	13	47	93	114	20	...	13	...	7	1	10	1
3. LUTHERANS ...	Europeans ...	73	65	8	1	...	...	59	...	2	...	...	2	...	1	...	1	6	1	...	...	...	...	...
	Anglo Indians.	11	3	8	...	1	...	3	...	2	...	...		...	...	...	...	5	...	...	...	...	...	...
	Indians ...	1,319	660	659	117	31	4	17	43	35	20	11	11	1	613	165	59	133	20	16	3	4	16	...
	TOTAL ...	*1,403*	728	675	118	32	4	79	43	39	20	11	13	1	614	165	60	144	21	16	3	4	16	...
4. METHODISTS.	Europeans ...	222	139	83	5	...	...	14	22	53	3	...	5	9	9	51	5	...	19	...	5	2	18	2
	Anglo Indians.	304	145	159	25	...	...	4	34	...	25	...	1	34	60	48	29	1	6	8	..	2	18	9
	Indians ...	1,221	515	706	25	24	4	8	61	8	37	7	3	29	181	190	27	..	281	13	27	104	177	15
	TOTAL ...	*1,747*	799	948	55	24	4	26	117	61	65	7	9	72	250	289	61	1	306	21	32	108	213	26

TABLE VIII.

Territorial Distribution of the Christian Population by Sect and Race—*continued*.

SECT.	RACE.	POPULATION RETURNED. Total.	Males.	Females.	POPULATION (BOTH SEXES) IN EACH DIVISION. I.	II.	III.	IV.	V.	VI.	VII.	VIII.	IX.	X.	XI.	XII.	XIII.	XIV.	XV.	XVI.	XVII.	XVIII.	XIX.	XX.
1	2	3	4	5	6	7	8	9	10	11	12	13	14	15	16	17	18	19	20	21	22	23	24	25
5. PRESBYTERIANS.	Europeans ...	293	170	123	11	...	1	43	10	8	...	...	13	6	14	23	38	61	39	3	3	4	15	1
	Anglo Indians.	154	68	86	4	1	...	...	3	1	5	...	4	3	10	34	51	6	1	23	3	5	...	...
	Indians ...	885	418	467	174	59	...	54	142	68	21	...	...	2	128	70	22	53	24	29	5	1	31	2
	TOTAL ...	*1,332*	656	676	189	60	1	97	155	77	26	...	17	11	152	127	111	120	64	55	11	10	46	3
6. ROMAN CATHOLICS.	Europeans ...	763	374	389	29	7	...	34	69	60	9	...	57	31	53	90	89	34	46	16	14	8	61	56
	Anglo Indians.	5,298	2,477	2,821	378	187	3	11	615	393	572	...	167	62	222	828	568	123	50	374	59	96	288	272
	Indians ...	18,944	9,166	9,778	3,785	583	188	97	1,131	984	821	20	206	395	1,278	1,592	2,122	237	924	1,074	126	215	1,475	1,691
	TOTAL ...	*25,005*	12,017	12,988	4,192	777	191	142	1,815	1,437	1,402	20	430	488	1,553	2,510	2,779	394	1,020	1,464	229	319	1,824	2,019
7. SYRIANS ...	Europeans ...	...	...	...	...	...	...	...	...	...	...	...	...	...	...	...	...	...	...	...	...	...	...	...
	Anglo Indians.	5	2	3	...	...	...	...	...	...	...	...	...	...	...	...	...	...	...	1	4	...	...	...
	Indians ...	110	106	4	4	3	...	31	23	...	...	...	1	...	...	33	13	...	...	2	...	...	...	...
	TOTAL ...	*115*	106	7	4	3	...	31	23	...	...	...	1	...	...	33	13	...	...	3	4	...	...	...
8. OTHERS ...	Europeans ...	218	156	62	1	...	1	16	26	2	1	...	1	3	13	13	36	38	52	2	5	1	7	...
	Anglo Indians.	155	69	86	3	...	2	...	22	6	10	...	5	...	22	21	36	13	4	4	6	...	1	...
	Indians ...	605	255	350	83	...	86	2	64	28	41	...	5	...	43	18	82	111	14	4	1	...	20	3
	TOTAL ...	*978*	480	498	87	...	89	18	112	36	52	...	11	3	78	52	154	162	70	10	12	1	28	3
	GRAND TOTAL ...	*41,812*	*20,582*	*21,230*	*5,271*	*1,151*	*327*	*540*	*2,672*	*2,421*	*1,891*	*90*	*962*	*815*	*4,176*	*5,144*	*4,176*	*1,372*	*2,141*	*2,356*	*483*	*572*	*2,806*	*2,446*

TABLE IX.

Infirmities by Age—(*a*) INSANE.

DIVISION.	TOTAL.			0—5.		5—10.		10—15.		15—20.		20—40.		40—55.		55—70.		70 and over.	
	Total.	Males.	Females.	Males.	Females.	Males.	Females.	Males.	Females.	Males.	Females.	Males.	Females.	Males.	Females.	Males.	Females.	Males.	Females.
1	2	3	4	5	6	7	8	9	10	11	12	13	14	15	16	17	18	19	20
I	1	1	...	...	...	...	...	...	...	...	...	1	...	...	...	...	...	...	...
II	8	7	1	...	...	...	...	1	...	2	...	3	1	1	...	...	...	...	...
III	1	...	1	...	...	...	...	...	...	...	...	...	...	...	...	...	1	...	...
IV	5	4	1	...	...	...	...	...	...	...	...	3	1	* 1	...	...	...	...	...
V	1	1	...	...	...	...	...	...	...	1	...	...	...	...	...	...	...	...	...
VI	3	3	...	...	...	...	...	...	...	...	...	2	...	1	...	...	...	...	...
VII	2	2	...	...	...	...	...	...	...	...	...	2	...	...	...	...	...	...	...
VIII	4	2	2	...	...	...	...	...	...	...	...	1	...	1	2	...	...	...	...
IX	4	3	1	...	...	...	...	...	...	1	...	2	...	...	...	...	1	...	...
X	5	4	1	...	...	...	...	...	...	...	...	4	...	...	1	...	...	...	...
XI	5	1	4	...	...	...	...	...	...	...	...	...	2	...	1	1	1	...	...
XII	4	3	1	...	...	...	...	...	...	1	1	1	...	...	...	...	...	1	...
XIII	1	1	...	...	...	...	...	...	...	...	...	1	...	...	...	...	...	...	...
XIV	547	405	142	...	...	...	...	2	2	7	3	188	71	148	52	54	9	6	5
XV	1	1	...	...	...	...	...	...	...	...	...	1	...	...	...	...	...	...	...
XVI	4	1	3	...	...	...	...	...	...	...	...	...	...	1	2	...	...	...	1
XVII	14	8	6	...	...	1	...	...	1	...	...	6	...	1	4	...	...	...	1
XVIII...	8	2	6	...	...	...	...	...	1	...	...	2	5	...	...	...	...	...	...
XIX	4	3	1	...	...	...	...	...	...	...	...	3	...	...	...	...	...	...	1
XX	3	...	3	...	...	...	...	...	...	...	1	...	2	...	...	...	...	...	...
TOTAL ...	*625*	*452*	*173*	...	...	1	...	3	4	12	5	220	82	154	62	55	12	7	8

* Also deaf-mute.

Infirmities by Age—(*b*) DEAF-MUTE.

DIVISION.	TOTAL.			0—5.		5—10.		10—15.		15—20.		20—40.		40—55.		55—70.		70 and over.	
	Total.	Males.	Females.	Males.	Females.	Males.	Females.	Males.	Females.	Males.	Females.	Males	Females.	Males.	Females	Males.	Females.	Males.	Females.
1	2	3	4	5	6	7	8	9	10	11	12	13	14	15	16	17	18	19	20
I	7	3	4	...	1	...	...	1	...	...	1	2	2	...	...	...	...	...	...
II	19	14	5	1	...	5	1	3	...	3	1*	1	2	1	1	...	...	...	...
III	9	8	1	...	...	1	...	...	1	1	...	4	...	1	...	...	...	1	...
IV	6	5	1	1	...	1	...	1	...	...	...	1	...	† 1	...	...	1	...	...
V	11	7	4	...	...	1	...	...	...	...	...	5	2	1	2	...	...	...	...
VI	4	4	...	...	...	2	...	...	...	...	...	1	...	...	...	...	...	1	...
VII	8	4	4	...	...	...	...	...	...	1	...	3	3	...	1	...	...	...	...
VIII	10	8	2	...	...	...	...	...	...	...	...	3	1	3	1	1	...	1	...
IX	5	5	...	...	...	...	...	...	...	...	...	2	...	3	...	...	...	...	...
X	12	8	4	1	...	3	1	2	...	1	2	...	...	...	1	1	...	...	...
XI	26	19	7	1	...	2	1	3	2	2	1	6	3	4	...	1	...	...	...
XII	18	11	7	...	1	1	2	2	...	4	2	4	1	...	1	...	...	...	...
XIII	6	3	3	...	...	...	1	2	...	...	...	...	2	1	...	...	...	...	...
XIV	...	...	...	...	...	...	...	...	...	...	...	...	...	...	...	...	...	...	...
XV	3	...	3	...	...	...	...	...	...	...	1	...	...	...	2	...	...	...	...
XVI	15	6	9	...	...	1	2	1	2	2	...	1	3	1	2	...	...	...	...
XVII	21	13	8	1	...	3	...	1	...	3	1	2	4	2	1	1	2	...	...
XVIII	6	3	3	...	...	...	1	...	1	...	...	...	...	1	1	2	...	...	...
XIX	8	6	2	...	...	...	...	1	1	1	...	...	...	3	1	1	...	...	...
XX	3	2	1	...	...	1	1	...	...	...	...	1	...	...	...	...	...	...	...
TOTAL ...	*197*	*129*	*68*	5	2	21	10	17	7	18	9	36	23	22	14	7	3	3	...

* Also leper.

† Also insane.

TABLE IX.

Infirmities by Age—(*c*) BLIND.

DIVISION.	TOTAL.			0—5.		5—10.		10—15.		15—20.		20—40.		40—55.		55—70.		70 and over.	
	Total.	Males.	Females.	Males.	Females.	Males.	Females.	Males.	Females.	Males.	Females.	Males.	Females.	Males.	Females.	Males.	Females.	Males.	Females.
1	2	3	4	5	6	7	8	9	10	11	12	13	14	15	16	17	18	19	20
I	3	1	2	...	...	...	...	...	...	...	...	...	1	..	...		1	1	...
II	28	18	10	1	...	1	...	1	...	1	...	2	3	3	4	7	2	2	1
III	4	1	3	...	...	...	...	...	...	...	1	1	1	...	...	...	1	...	...
IV	7	2	5	..	1	...	...	.	...	1	...	1	...	...	2	...	2	..	...
V	10	5	5	...	...	...	...	1	...	1	1	1	..	...	1	1	2	1	1
VI	1	1	...	...	...	...	...	...	...	..	...	...	...	1	...	..	...	..	...
VII	5	1	4	..	...	...	...	...	..	...	...	...	1	..	...	...	2	1	1
VIII	7	4	3	...	1	...	...	...	...		1	3	...	..	...	1	1	...	...
IX	3	2	1	...	..	...	...	...	...	...	...	1	...	...	...	1	1	...	...
X	3	1	2	...	.	...	...	...	...		...	...	...	...	2	...		1	...
XI	16	7	9	...	...	...	...	1	1	1	1	...	1	2	3	1	2	2	1
XII	7	3	4	...	...	...	...	...	.	...	...	2	3	1	...	...	...	...	1
XIII	8	3	5	...	1	...	...	...	...	...	...	...	...	1	3	...	...	2	1
XIV	5	3	2	...	...	...	...	...	1	...	...	2	...	...	...		...	1	1
XV	3	2	1	...	...	.	...	...	...	...	...	1	..	...	...	1	...	...	1
XVI	12	6	6		...	...	...	1	1	...	...	2	2	2	...	...	...	1	3
XVII	13	7	6	...	...	...	..	...	1	...	...	3	1	1	...	2	3	1	1
XVIII	15	8	7	...	...	...	...	...	..	1	...	1	1	2	3	1	2	3	1
XIX	15	7	8	1	...		..		...	...	...	...	2	4	3	..	2	2	1
XX	10	5	5	...		1	1	...	1	...	...	...	...	1	1	2	...	1	2
TOTAL ...	*175*	*87*	*88*	2	3	2	1	4	5	5	4	20	16	18	22	17	21	19	16

Infirmities by Age—(*d*) LEPER.

DIVISION.	TOTAL.			0—5.		5—10.		10—15.		15—20.		20—40.		40—55.		55—70.		70 and over.	
	Total.	Males.	Females.	Males.	Females.	Males.	Females.	Males.	Females.	Males.	Females.	Males.	Females.	Males.	Females.	Males.	Females.	Males.	Females.
1	2	3	4	5	6	7	8	9	10	11	12	13	14	15	16	17	18	19	20
I	5	5	...	...		1	..	..	...	1	..	2	...	1	...	...	...	...	...
II	171	126	45	.	...	3	1	4	2	8	*4	67	22	33	11	11	4	...	1
III	4	2	2	...	1	...	...	...	...	...		..	1	1	...	1	...	...	...
IV	1	1	..	...	..	...	...	...	...	...	...	1	..	...	...	...	...	...	...
V	1	..	1	...	...	...	...	...	...	...	...	...	...	..	..	...	1	...	...
VI	1	1	...	...	..	..	.	...	...	...	...	1	...	...	...	...	...	...	...
VII	1	1	...	...	...	...	...	...	...	...	...	...	...	1	...	...	...	...	...
VIII	9	8	1	..	...	...	...	1	...	...	...	4	...	3	1	...	...	...	...
IX	2	2	...	...	...	...	...	...	...	...	...	2		...	..	...	...	...	...
X	5	4	1	...	...	...	...	...	...	..	...	1	1	2	...	...	...	1	...
XI	13	10	3	...	...	...	...	...	...	1	...	4	...	3	2	2	1	...	...
XII	4	1	3	...	...	.	...	...	..	..	...	1	2		1	...	...	...	...
XIII	3	3	...	.	...		...	...	...	..	...	2	...	1	..	...	...	...	...
XIV	1	1	...	...	...	...	..	...	...	...	...	1	...	...	..	...	...	..	...
XV	2	2	...	...	..	...	...	...	...	...	...	...	...	2	...	...	.	...	...
XVI	10	6	4	...	...	...	...	...	...	...	...	5	2	1	1	...	1	...	...
XVII	9	6	3	...	...	...	...	...	...	...	...	5	1	1	2	...	...	...	...
XVIII	14	11	3	...		...	...	...	1	2	.	7	1	2	1	...	..	...	...
XIX	10	7	3	...	..	.	...	...	...	1	...	5	3	...	...	1	...	...	...
XX	6	3	3	..	...	...	...	...	..	.	3	...	...	2	...	1	...	...	...
TOTAL ...	*272*	*200*	*72*	...	1	4	1	5	3	13	7	108	33	53	19	16	7	1	1

* One of these was also deaf-mute.

TABLE X.

Occupation.

Group No.	DESCRIPTION OF OCCUPATION.	POPULATION SUPPORTED.						ACTUAL WORKERS (BOTH SEXES) BY DIVISIONS.																			
		Total workers and dependents.	Total actual workers.		Partially agriculturists.		Dependents.	I.	II.	III.	IV.	V.	VI.	VII.	VIII.	IX.	X.	XI.	XII.	XIII.	XIV.	XV.	XVI.	XVII.	XVIII.	XIX.	XX.
			Males.	Females.	Males.	Females.																					
1	2	3	4	5	6	7	8	9	10	11	12	13	14	15	16	17	18	19	20	21	22	23	24	25	26	27	28
	CLASS A.—PRODUCTION OF RAW MATERIALS.																										
	ORDER 1.—PASTURE AND AGRICULTURE.																										
1-A	Non-cultivating landowner	5,787	1,396	466	...	...	3,925	13	46	37	51	81	73	235	194	128	22	71	66	93	15	27	80	108	251	113	158
1-B	Non-cultivating tenant	73	47	1	...	...	25	...	1	...	...	...	1	...	1	...	...	1	...	...	...	...	1	36	...	6	1
2-A	Cultivating landowner	6,916	2,291	213	...	...	4,412	97	116	33	40	113	70	146	130	202	197	121	92	129	41	80	140	85	211	262	199
2-B	Cultivating tenant	2,282	1,047	87	...	...	1,148	7	110	99	193	7	8	50	10	22	101	76	13	19	10	24	17	21	29	116	202
3	Agents, managers of landed estates (not planters), clerks, rent collectors, etc. ...	457	138	19	3	...	300	1	...	1	...	3	4	4	2	1	2	10	2	4	2	18	15	24	32	22	10
4	Farm servants and field labourers	2,187	727	251	...	...	1,209	61	53	137	2	23	4	15	11	7	155	26	9	5	23	56	9	23	10	97	252
5	Tea, coffee, cinchona and indigo plantations	91	18	1	...	...	72	1	2	...	1	...	...	1	...	...	...	1	5	...	1	2	1	...	1	3	...
6	Fruit, flower, vegetable, betel, vine, areca-nut, etc., growers	6,086	2,032	165	7	...	3,889	40	341	130	13	4	8	9	14	4	101	3	192	87	149	233	18	45	97	429	280
7	Forest officers, rangers, guards, etc. ...	163	27	2	...	...	134	...	...	...	...	1	...	2	2	1	1	...	3	1	3	...	...	2	8	4	1
8	Wood-cutters; fire-wood, lac, catechu, rubber, etc., collectors and charcoal burners...	763	144	350	...	...	269	10	30	16	7	6	5	15	19	7	12	75	9	26	27	9	13	13	27	110	58
9	Cattle and buffalo breeders and keepers ...	504	174	29	1	...	301	1	5	1	...	1	11	1	15	5	19	18	19	20	7	8	1	14	18	24	15
10	Sheep, goat and pig breeders	36	23	4	...	...	9	...	...	...	...	...	...	...	...	1	3	4	...	...	17	...	...	1	...	...	1
11	Breeders of other animals (horses, mules, camels, asses, etc.)	31	8	...	...	...	23	...	...	1	...	2	...	...	...	...	1	...	...	...	...	2	2	...	...	...	...
12	Herdsmen, shepherds, goatherds, etc. ...	263	107	16	2	...	140	1	5	18	2	3	3	4	32	1	5	8	4	1	1	2	4	3	11	5	10
13	Keepers of birds, bees, silkworms, etc. ...	3	1	...	...	...	2	...	...	...	...	...	...	...	...	...	...	...	...	...	...	...	...	1	...	...	...
	ORDER 2.—FISHING AND HUNTING.																										
14	Fishing	5,045	1,864	77	...	...	3,104	527	38	13	6	...	...	16	7	...	13	16	2	1	1	7	36	15	577	341	325
15	Hunting	29	9	...	...	...	20	...	...	1	...	...	...	3	...	...	...	1	...	...	1	...	...	...	...	...	3
	ORDER 3.—MINES.																										
16	Coal mines and petroleum wells	37	10	2	...	...	25	1	2	...	5	...	...	...	...	...	...	...	...	2	...	...	...	...	1	...	1
17	Mines and metallic minerals (gold, iron, manganese, etc.)	78	13	1	...	...	64	...	...	...	...	1	...	2	1	5	1	3	...	...	...	...	...	1	...	...	...
	ORDER 4.—QUARRIES OF HARD ROCKS.																										
18	Other minerals (jade, diamonds, limestone, etc.)	30	7	...	1	...	23	...	...	1	2	...	...	2	...	...	...	...	...	...	...	...	1	...	...	...	1
	ORDER 5.—SALT, ETC.																										
19	Rock, sea and marsh salt	16	3	...	...	...	13	...	...	...	...	1	...	...	...	...	...	...	...	...	...	1	1	...	...	...	...
20	Extraction of saltpetre, alum and other substances soluble in water	2	...	1	...	...	1	...	...	...	...	...	...	...	...	...	...	...	1	...	...	...	...	...	...	...	...

TABLE X.

Occupation—*continued.*

Group No.	DESCRIPTION OF OCCUPATION.	POPULATION SUPPORTED. Total workers and dependents.	Total actual workers. Males.	Total actual workers. Females.	Partially agriculturists. Males.	Partially agriculturists. Females.	Dependents.	ACTUAL WORKERS (BOTH SEXES) BY DIVISIONS. I.	II.	III.	IV.	V.	VI.	VII.	VIII.	IX.	X.	XI.	XII.	XIII.	XIV.	XV.	XVI.	XVII.	XVIII.	XIX.	XX.
1	2	3	4	5	6	7	8	9	10	11	12	13	14	15	16	17	18	19	20	21	22	23	24	25	26	27	28
	CLASS B.—PREPARATION AND SUPPLY OF MATERIAL SUBSTANCES.																										
	ORDER 6.—TEXTILES.																										
21	Cotton ginning, cleaning and pressing ...	499	326	13	...	...	160	...	...	...	...	...	19	8	1	...	275	8	20	1	...	3	4	...	...	...	...
22	Cotton spinning, sizing and weaving ...	22,338	8,811	890	21	4	12,637	206	671	604	10	20	306	250	99	84	2,599	2,183	441	71	180	2	51	65	883	204	772
23	Jute spinning, pressing and weaving ...	63	22	2	...	...	39	2	5	3	3	...	...	2	...	5	...	...	2	...	...	...	1	...	1	...	...
24	Rope, twine and string	74	27	17	...	..	30	5	3	2	4	3	3	1	...	...	1	..	...	...	...	...	...	7	1	1	13
25	Other fibres (cocoanut, aloes, flax, hemp, straw, etc.)	24	8	...	...	...	16	...	...	...	...	...	...	...	...	...	...	...	...	...	...	...	8	...	.	..	...
26	Wool carders and spinners, weavers of woollen blankets, carpets, etc.	55	20	3	...	...	32	...	18	...	...	...	...	...	2	...	...	...	...	...	...	...	...	3	...	...	...
27	Silk spinners and weavers	999	409	82	...	...	508	...	3	...	1	...	29	...	2	8	...	52	7	13	...	...	14	12	...	...	350
28	Hair, camel and horse hair, bristles work, brush makers, etc.	58	13	1	...	...	44	...	...	...	...	1		12	...			...	...	...	...	...	...	...	...	1	...
* 30	Dyeing, bleaching, printing, preparation and sponging of textiles	885	304	21	1	..	560	3	73	26	3	1	3	6	4	4	20	30	3	7	1	2	7	84	21	19	8
31	Other (lace, crape, embroideries, fringes, etc.), and insufficiently described textile industries	2,594	860	107	...	...	1,627	...	..	...	16	...	2	1	4	...	8	50	9	80	6	15	20	400	125	229	2
	ORDER 7.—HIDES, SKINS AND HARD MATERIALS FROM THE ANIMAL KINGDOM.																										
32	Tanners, curriers, leather dressers, etc. ...	826	282	11	...	1	533	46	93	52	8	16	40	13	3	1	8	1	9	...	...	2	...	...	1	..	...
33	Maker of leather articles, such as trunks, waterbags, etc.	27	5	..	..	...	23	...		2	...	...	1	...	...	...	...	...	1	...	1	...	...	..	...	..	...
34	Furriers	5	2	...	...	...	3	..	...	...	..	...	..	...	...	...	...	...	...	...	...	2	...	...	...	..	...
35	Bone, ivory, horn, shell, etc., workers ...	20	3	4	...	...	13	...	...	6		...	...	...	...	...	...	...	...	..	...	...	...	...	...	1	...
	ORDER 8.—WOOD.																										
36	Sawyers, carpenters, turners and joiners, etc.	11,818	4,199	37	18	1	7,582	116	361	86	115	210	94	315	80	315	60	648	127	188	46	91	470	309	206	263	136
37	Basket makers and other industries of woody material, including leaves	697	200	107	1	...	390	...	11	18	2	2	61	24	31	30	21	4	18	4	2	16	11	13	14	25	..
	ORDER 9.—METALS.																										
38	Forging and rolling of iron and other metals.	450	150	3	...	..	297	2	55	14	3	7	13	7	1	11	3	12	2	9	3	...	...	1	2	8	...
39	Plough and agricultural implement makers.	1	...	...	...	...	1	...	...	...	..	...	...	...	...	...	...	...	...	...	...	...	...	...	...	...	...
40	Makers of arms, guns, etc.	642	202	5	1	...	435	4	5	...	1	1	4	11	4	7	11	2	69	28	...	2	36	8	6	7	1
41	Other workers in iron and makers of implements and tools, principally or exclusively of iron	4,550	1,657	15	2	...	2,878	32	195	74	19	27	34	67	47	153	85	270	97	93	36	29	179	121	48	54	12
42	Workers in brass, copper and bell metal ...	1,407	401	7	...	...	999	...	4	10	5	3	3	8	3	29	4	60	3	13	6	4	49	94	96	13	1

* No persons were returned under group 29.

TABLE X.

Occupation—*continued.*

Group No.	DESCRIPTION OF OCCUPATION.	POPULATION SUPPORTED. Total workers and dependents.	Total actual workers. Males.	Total actual workers. Females.	Partially agriculturists. Males.	Partially agriculturists. Females.	Dependents.	ACTUAL WORKERS (BOTH SEXES) BY DIVISIONS. I.	II.	III.	IV.	V.	VI.	VII.	VIII.	IX.	X.	XI.	XII.	XIII.	XIV.	XV.	XVI.	XVII.	XVIII.	XIX.	XX.
1	2	3	4	5	6	7	8	9	10	11	12	13	14	15	16	17	18	19	20	21	22	23	24	25	26	27	28
	CLASS B.—PREPARATION AND SUPPLY OF MATERIAL SUBSTANCES—*cont.*																										
	ORDER 9.—METALS—*cont.*																										
43	Workers in other metals (tin, zinc, lead, quick-silver, etc.)	2,464	894	13	1	...	1,557	41	87	23	43	52	51	63	48	25	22	109	19	36	7	23	76	83	50	42	7
44	Die-sinkers, etc.	3	2	...	...	...	1	...	1	...	...	...	...	...	...	1	...	...	...	...	...	...	...	...	...	...	...
	ORDER 10.—CERAMICS.																										
45	Makers of glass and crystal ware	193	63	4	1	...	126	3	2	...	...	...	1	...	5	4	2	2	...	2	...	1	11	8	8	17	1
46	Makers of porcelain and crockery	136	73	7	...	...	56	...	...	...	...	...	...	...	1	...	7	...	...	...	...	...	...	...	72	...	...
47	Potters and earthen pipe and bowl makers.	687	208	84	...	...	395	...	39	1	...	...	...	...	...	1	17	94	2	1	9	...	1	3	44	79	1
48	Brick and tile makers	433	124	88	3	1	221	...	...	1	...	1	...	...	...	...	2	14	1	2	169	8	10	2	...	1	1
49	Others (mosaic, talc, mica, alabaster, etc., workers)	14	2	..	...	...	12	..	...	...	...	...	...	...	...	...	...	...	1	...	...	...	...	1	...	...	...
	ORDER 11.—CHEMICAL PRODUCTS PROPERLY SO CALLED, AND ANALOGOUS.																										
50	Manufacture of matches and explosive materials	78	25	1	...	...	52	1	...	...	...	3	...	2	1	...	3	1	...	...	...	...	...	1	8	5	1
51	Manufacture of aerated and mineral waters.	190	73	1	...	...	116	...	9	2	4	5	4	7	3	2	3	...	8	1	...	1	3	12	8	2	...
52	Manufacture of dyes, paint and ink	351	97	3	3	...	251	...	19	4	6	2	7	11	17	1	...	1	2	...	...	...	1	26	2	1	...
53	Manufacture and refining of vegetable and mineral oils	598	242	8	2	...	348	3	104	6	1	23	5	19	15	...	...	19	17	1		2	1	2	24	8	...
54	Manufacture of paper, cardboard and paper maché	18	8	2	...	...	8	...	1	...	...	...	1	...	...	...	3	2	1	...	1	...	...	1	...	...	...
55	Others (soap, candles, lac, cutch, perfumes and miscellaneous drugs)	65	13	5	...	..	47	.	1	...	1	...	3	...	...	...	...	1	3	...	...	1	...	6	1	1	...
	ORDER 12.—FOOD INDUSTRIES.																										
56	Rice pounders and huskers and flour grinders	2,651	265	1,623	2	...	763	20	1,612	43	1	7	6	13	28	10	21	44	9	...	1	1	1	12	7	5	47
57	Bakers and biscuit makers	2,918	601	816	2	...	1,501	55	141	11	42	34	120	52	67	74	98	115	97	45	24	20	49	109	85	144	35
58	Grain parchers, etc.	14	...	4	...	...	10	...	1	...	...	..	...	..	...	...	...	3	...	...	..	..	...	...	...	...	...
59	Butchers	2,717	839	116	1	...	1,762	34	73	20	14	3	121	41	3	1	121	126	44	26	19	6	88	39	95	68	13
60	Fish curers	39	2	5	...	...	32	...	.	...	...	..	...	...	...	...	...	5	1	...	...	...	1	...	...	...	...
61	Butter, cheese and ghee makers	6	2	...	...	...	4	...	1	...	...	...	...	...	...	...	...	1	...	...	...	...	...	...	...	...	...
62	Makers of sugar, molasses and gur	58	28	1	...	...	29	...	3	...	...	3	1	2	11	2	1	2	...	...	...	...	...	1	1	...	2
63	Sweetmeat makers, preparers of jam and condiments, etc.	476	86	154	2	...	236	2	10	...	2	5	15	1	5	10	5	11	9	8	23	68	1	16	15	8	26
64	Brewers and distillers	14	7	...	...	...	7	...	4	...	...	...	...	...	...	...	1	...	...	...	1	...	...	...	1	...	...
65	Toddy drawers	3,842	1,267	15	13	...	2,560	2	268	224	...	2	15	...	...	2	37	4	3	4	49	45	2	11	17	326	271
66	Manufacturers of tobacco, opium and ganja.	1,308	487	95	1	...	726	10	154	143	10	18	65	26	14	5	53	2	3	21	3	1	4	23	18	6	3

TABLE X.

Occupation—*continued*.

Group No.	DESCRIPTION OF OCCUPATION.	POPULATION SUPPORTED. Total workers and dependents.	Total actual workers. Males.	Total actual workers. Females.	Partially agriculturist. Males.	Partially agriculturist. Females.	Dependents.	ACTUAL WORKERS (BOTH SEXES) BY DIVISIONS. I.	II.	III.	IV.	V.	VI.	VII.	VIII.	IX.	X.	XI.	XII.	XIII.	XIV.	XV.	XVI.	XVII.	XVIII.	XIX.	XX.
1	2	3	4	5	6	7	8	9	10	11	12	13	14	15	16	17	18	19	20	21	22	23	24	25	26	27	28
	CLASS B.—PREPARATION AND SUPPLY OF MATERIAL SUBSTANCES—*cont.*																										
	ORDER 13.—INDUSTRIES OF DRESS AND THE TOILET.																										
67	Hat, cap and turban makers	204	70	6	...	..	128	2	8	...	6	2	7	36	...	...	...	...	...	1	...		3	3	5	3	...
68	Tailors, milliners, dress makers and darners, embroiderers on linen	11,369	3,910	660	2	...	6,799	259	231	67	473	85	156	121	44	20	59	178	146	97	3	131	113	1,329	434	528	86
69	Shoe, boot and sandal makers	3,522	1,130	99	3	...	2,293	23	16	42	7	6	20	...	3	...	600	23	106	66	8	66	5	172	14	45	7
70	Other industries pertaining to dress-gloves, socks, gaiters, belts, buttons, umbrellas, canes, etc.	146	53	7	...	...	86	1	5	9		1	5	5	5	...	6	3	...	...	2	1	6	6	2	2	1
71	Washing, cleaning and dyeing	4,308	1,384	411	6	1	2,508	64	410	64	13	32	22	89	17	30	122	77	108	49	204	76	58	68	31	166	95
72	Barbers, hair-dressers and wigmakers ...	3,409	1,262	24	3	...	2,123	23	152	32	9	56	88	117	103	7	65	165	53	44	7	29	53	80	73	72	58
73	Other industries connected with the toilet (tattooers, shampooers, bath-houses, etc.).	74	25	20	1	...	29	...	22	7	2	1	1	5	2	...	...	...	5	...	...	...	18	...	...	...	...
	ORDER 14.—FURNITURE INDUSTRIES.																										
74	Cabinet makers, carriage painters, etc. ...	541	150	9	4	...	382	1	10	...	...	3	3	2	7	9	1	36	10	7	1	8	...	23	8	10	2
	ORDER 15.—BUILDING INDUSTRIES.																										
* 76	Lime burners, cement workers	1,092	327	156	2	...	609	11	30	297	3	2	3	13	1	...	21	9	1	5	5	2	28	9	3	39	1
77	Excavators, plinth builders and well sinkers.	190	69	43	1	...	78	...	3	5	23	...	...	...	1	...	19	2	1	1	52	...	...	...	...	5	...
78	Stone and marble workers, masons and bricklayers	10,667	3,586	500	11	...	6,581	44	400	119	21	57	92	301	201	29	182	442	155	122	228	110	216	308	267	593	199
79	Others (thatchers, building contractors, house painters, tilers, plumbers, locksmiths, etc.)	1,068	358	8	2	...	702	8	30	2	17	8	14	8	18	8	5	72	11	28	1	3	14	25	25	42	27
	ORDER 16.—CONSTRUCTION OF MEANS OF TRANSPORT.																										
80	Cart, carriage, palki, etc., makers and wheelwrights	623	204	4	5	...	415	1	5	2	1	4	12	4	4	1	9	14	12	19	1	6	34	40	22	13	4
81	Saddlers, harness makers, whip and lash makers	421	128	1		...	292	1	...	...	...	...	2	1	...	...	30	1	1	29	...	...	3	56	4	1	...
82	Ship and boat builders	45	29	1	..	...	15	...	9	3	3	...	2	1	...	...	...	...	...	...	...	...	3	...	...	9	...
	ORDER 17.—PRODUCTION AND TRANSMISSION OF PHYSICAL FORCES (HEAT, LIGHT, ELECTRICITY, MOTIVE POWER, ETC.).																										
83	Gas works, electric light and ice factories	1,051	369	13	2	...	669	1	8	2	4	4	10	10	13	16	59	29	85	29	15	7	28	40	5	10	7

* No persons were returned under group 75.

TABLE X.

Occupation—*continued.*

Group No.	DESCRIPTION OF OCCUPATION.	POPULATION SUPPORTED. Total workers and dependants.	Total actual workers. Males.	Total actual workers. Females.	Partially agriculturists. Males.	Partially agriculturists. Females.	Dependants.	ACTUAL WORKERS (BOTH SEXES) BY DIVISIONS. I.	II.	III.	IV.	V.	VI.	VII.	VIII.	IX.	X.	XI.	XII.	XIII.	XIV.	XV.	XVI.	XVII.	XVIII.	XIX.	XX.
1	2	3	4	5	6	7	8	9	10	11	12	13	14	15	16	17	18	19	20	21	22	23	24	25	26	27	28
	CLASS B.—PREPARATION AND SUPPLY OF MATERIAL SUBSTANCES—*cont.*																										
	ORDER 18.—INDUSTRIES OF LUXURY AND THOSE PERTAINING TO LITERATURE AND THE ARTS AND SCIENCES.																										
84	Printers, lithographers, engravers, etc. ...	12,308	4,733	29	32	...	7,546	131	274	102	60	147	229	713	324	71	69	671	333	223	25	120	285	329	220	261	175
85	Newspaper and magazine managers and editors, journalists, etc.	430	156	1	3	..	273	12	6	1	8	9	11	13	18	1	..	3	7	7	...	13	...	10	23	7	8
86	Bookbinders and stitchers, envelope makers, etc.	2,626	1,204	7	6		1,415	57	51	12	2	21	43	173	100	34	8	198	83	31	4	62	148	56	31	77	20
87	Makers of musical instruments ...	57	15	...	...	...	42	1	...	...	...	...	...	...	...		...	1	...	...	...	...	5	3	4	1	...
88	Makers of watches and clocks and optical, photographic and surgical instruments ...	744	225	2	...	...	517	7	10	1	5	18	13	7	9	5	5	12	8	15	...	6	14	45	15	15	17
89	Workers in precious stones and metals, enamellers, imitation jewellery makers, gilders, etc.	13,112	4,361	63	27	...	8,688	42	281	78	174	122	67	373	195	648	90	495	102	251	14	49	330	529	344	183	57
90	Makers of bangles, rosaries, bead and other necklaces, spangles, lingams and sacred threads	107	45	9	1	...	53	...	2	1	...	...	5	8	2	1	2	2	2	...	...	...	10	22	...	2	...
91	Toy, kite, cage, fishing tackle, etc., makers, taxidermists, etc.	193	50	17	...	...	126	2	1	2	1	2	23	3	4	2	1	1	3	1	1	6	2	6	1	5	...
92	Others, including managers, persons other than performers employed in theatres and other places of public entertainment, employés of public societies, race course service, huntsmen, etc.	519	235	18	6	...	266	2	2	...	2	...	68	4	18	...	1	2	29	26	...	6	9	22	27	17	18
	ORDER 19.—INDUSTRIES CONCERNED WITH REFUSE MATTER.																										
93	Sweepers, scavengers, dust and sweeping contractors	4,045	1,067	1,621	...	1	1,357	26	549	166	66	26	20	61	326	15	10	50	138	501	16	41	23	18	32	552	52
	ORDER 20.—TRANSPORT BY WATER.																										
94	Harbour works, dockyards and pilots ...	4,660	1,722	118	16	1	2,820	370	435	44	172	173	171	193	39	18	29	37	45	22	2	...	21	28	18	11	12
95	Ship-owners and their employés, ship-brokers, ships' officers, engineers, mariners and firemen	1662	357	5	...	...	300	48	17	10	151	75	12	29	2	1	...	1	1	...	3	2	1	4	...	4	1
96	Persons employed on the maintenance of streams, rivers and canals (including construction)	39	14	1	...	...	24	...	1	...	...	...	...	1	...	..	...	...	...	...	...	...	2	1	2	3	5
97	Boat owners, boatmen and tow men ...	5,416	1,898	24	1	1	3,494	1,646	13	...	49	13	9	9	1	1	...	1	4	2	1	9	1	107	...	6	50

TABLE X.

Occupation—*continued.*

Group No.	Description of occupation.	Population supported: Total workers and dependants.	Total actual workers: Males.	Total actual workers: Females.	Partially agriculturists: Males.	Partially agriculturists: Females.	Dependants.	Actual workers (both sexes) by divisions: I.	II.	III.	IV.	V.	VI.	VII.	VIII.	IX.	X.	XI.	XII.	XIII.	XIV.	XV.	XVI.	XVII	XVIII	XIX.	XX.
1	2	3	4	5	6	7	8	9	10	11	12	13	14	15	16	17	18	19	20	21	22	23	24	25	26	27	28
	CLASS B.—PREPARATION AND SUPPLY OF MATERIAL SUBSTANCES—*cont.*																										
	ORDER 21.—TRANSPORT BY ROAD.																										
98	Persons employed on the construction and maintenance of roads and bridges ...	3,708	1,318	722	7	...	1,668	1	10	183	17	13	7	36	4	10	50	437	8	2	962	1	...	13	10	221	55
99	Cart owners and drivers, coachmen, stable boys, tramway, mail carriage, etc., managers and employés (excluding private servants)	18,781	7,012	189	58	1	11,580	76	1,553	262	150	138	249	377	359	152	185	675	521	245	124	271	571	496	242	445	115
100	Palki, etc., bearers and owners	815	354	11	...	...	450	18	20	...	12	22	18	12	13	18	3	...	52	92	...	...	3	56	5	12	9
101	Pack elephant, camel, mule, ass and bullock owners and drivers	5	2	1	...	...	2	...	...	...	...	...	...	...	...	...	...	...	...	1	...	...	1	1	...	...	...
102	Porters and messengers	2,552	878	270	2	...	1,404	88	560	83	121	4	14	45	30	19	10	10	19	42	12	7	58	17	16	31	12
	ORDER 22.—TRANSPORT BY RAIL.																										
103	Railway employés of all kinds other than construction coolies	16,607	5,214	50	90	...	11,343	228	510	220	103	194	208	512	188	156	567	71	446	396	92	43	333	130	136	63	27
104	Labourers employed on railway construction.	838	286	18	...	...	534	17	68	17	...	...	6	8	12	16	67	1	26	16	35	4	9	1	...	1	...
	ORDER 23.—POST OFFICE, TELEGRAPH AND TELEPHONE SERVICES.																										
105	Post office, Telegraph and Telephone services	6,524	1,958	55	59	...	4,511	31	84	32	82	147	162	286	165	57	31	152	125	90	27	18	129	140	103	85	67
	ORDER 24.—BANKS, ESTABLISHMENTS OF CREDIT, EXCHANGE AND INSURANCE.																										
106	Bank managers, money-lenders, exchange and insurance agents, money changers and brokers, and their employés	5,295	1,688	412	53	2	3,195	14	30	6	94	120	155	238	322	276	32	70	189	34	5	44	45	66	190	68	102
	ORDER 25.—BROKERAGE, COMMISSION AND EXPORT.																										
107	Brokers, commission agents, commercial travellers, warehouse owners and employés	4,270	1,235	23	38	...	3,012	30	58	15	120	97	142	166	212	89	18	28	63	23	14	4	30	68	43	22	16
	ORDER 26.—TRADE IN TEXTILES.																										
108	Trade in piece-goods, wool, cotton, silk, hair and other textiles	6,248	1,997	85	60	...	4,166	23	114	9	115	49	301	117	429	381	24	113	128	43	3	4	94	39	38	29	29
	ORDER 27.—TRADE IN SKINS, LEATHER, AND FURS.																										
109	Trade in skins, leather, furs, feathers, horn, etc.	1,736	618	13	19	...	1,105	12	42	6	183	88	25	18	14	3	23	6	186	2	6	3	20	23	13	7	1

TABLE X.

Occupation—*continued.*

Group No.	DESCRIPTION OF OCCUPATION.	POPULATION SUPPORTED. Total workers and dependants.	Total actual workers. Males.	Total actual workers. Females.	Partially agriculturists. Males.	Partially agriculturists. Females.	Dependants.	ACTUAL WORKERS (BOTH SEXES) BY DIVISIONS. I.	II.	III.	IV.	V.	VI.	VII.	VIII.	IX.	X.	XI.	XII.	XIII.	XIV.	XV.	XVI.	XVII.	XVIII.	XIX.	XX.
1	2	3	4	5	6	7	8	9	10	11	12	13	14	15	16	17	18	19	20	21	22	23	24	25	26	27	28
	CLASS B.—PREPARATION AND SUPPLY OF MATERIAL SUBSTANCES—*cont.*																										
	ORDER 28.—TRADE IN WOOD.																										
110	Trade in wood (not firewood), cork, bark, etc.	1,550	419	28	18	1	1,103	24	54	7	60	34	15	30	42	38	13	18	59	6	4	1	7	21	9	4	1
	ORDER 29.—TRADE IN METALS.																										
111	Trade in metals, machinery, knife, tool, etc., sellers	496	141	4	2	...	351	1	7	...	14	5	13	12	24	8	1	13	5	14	1	3	10	3	5	5	1
	ORDER 30.—TRADE IN POTTERY.																										
112	Trade in pottery	75	11	16	...	...	48	1	1	...	...	...	...	2	...	...	...	1	1	...	...	...	7	..	12	1	1
	ORDER 31.—TRADE IN CHEMICAL PRODUCTS.																										
113	Trade in chemical products (drugs, dyes, paints, petroleum, explosives, etc.) ...	1,761	516	39	4	...	1,206	31	85	20	10	21	18	63	63	48	7	53	23	10	4	10	3	47	30	7	2
	ORDER 32.—HOTELS, CAFÉS, RESTAURANTS, ETC.																										
114	Vendors of wine, liquors, ærated waters, etc.	4,324	1,334	61	28	2	2,929	43	208	119	7	21	51	54	52	16	57	181	74	15	25	11	63	61	51	230	56
115	Owners and managers of hotels, cookshops, sarais, etc., and their employés	2,237	752	143	15	2	1,342	8	26	5	68	66	41	45	127	47	20	23	55	56	10	12	27	84	93	58	24
	ORDER 33.—OTHER TRADE IN FOOD STUFFS.																										
116	Fish dealers	2,992	480	1,241	2	...	1,271	619	62	11	2	2	5	83	14	7	10	125	20	7	7	4	53	28	313	145	204
117	Grocers and sellers of vegetable oil, salt and other condiments	10,598	2,964	678	54	2	6,956	103	261	89	138	194	241	274	494	185	101	177	189	84	60	44	167	253	244	251	93
118	Sellers of milk, butter, ghee, poultry, eggs, etc.	4,938	1,321	556	19	...	3,061	42	113	30	38	71	91	171	147	123	32	182	111	84	12	83	87	158	119	109	74
119	Sellers of sweetmeats, sugar, gur and molasses	4,800	830	1,582	11	...	2,388	121	180	83	73	123	102	207	129	54	58	167	128	129	1	25	218	285	118	123	88
120	Cardamom, betel-leaf, vegetables, fruit, and areca nut sellers	7,158	1,788	1,319	28	1	4,051	81	258	127	90	93	256	279	263	152	108	176	126	250	30	37	109	208	158	226	80
121	Grain and pulse dealers	7,307	1,911	456	31	1	4,940	38	705	17	69	43	234	81	147	122	53	129	80	57	5	15	118	114	174	96	70
122	Tobacco, opium, ganja, etc., sellers	2,433	826	65	7	...	1,542	5	76	88	30	78	86	83	63	24	45	65	24	18	6	12	28	70	46	29	15
123	Dealers in sheep, goats and pigs	644	154	48	2	...	442	24	34	1	8	1	18	13	8	5	35	15	8	11	3	...	2	...	13	3	...
124	Dealers in hay, grass and fodder	290	26	126	...	...	138	1	3	26	...	2	5	1	2	...	1	2	10	6	16	14	7	5	10	41	...

TABLE X.

Occupation—*continued.*

Group No.	Description of Occupation.	Population Supported: Total workers and dependants.	Total actual workers: Males.	Total actual workers: Females.	Partially agriculturists: Males.	Partially agriculturists: Females.	Dependants.	Actual Workers (both sexes) by Divisions: I.	II.	III.	IV.	V.	VI.	VII.	VIII.	IX.	X.	XI.	XII.	XIII.	XIV.	XV.	XVI.	XVII.	XVIII.	XIX.	XX.
1	2	3	4	5	6	7	8	9	10	11	12	13	14	15	16	17	18	19	20	21	22	23	24	25	26	27	28
	CLASS B.—PREPARATION AND SUPPLY OF MATERIAL SUBSTANCES—*cont.*																										
	ORDER 34.—TRADE IN CLOTHING AND TOILET ARTICLES.																										
125	Trade in ready-made clothing and other articles of dress and the toilet (hats, umbrellas, socks, ready-made shoes, perfumes, etc.)	2,825	814	36	4	...	1,975	1	4	44	61	41	78	13	48	13	8	28	5	19	1	3	38	279	135	13	18
	ORDER 35.—TRADE IN FURNITURE.																										
126	Trade in furniture, carpets, curtains and bedding	332	92	12	2	...	228	1	2	9	2	5	17	20	12	16	...	8	1	...	...	...	2	4	5	...	...
127	Hardware, cooking utensils, porcelain, crockery, glassware, bottles, articles for gardening, the cellar, etc.	2,200	771	19	2	...	1,410	2	56	2	54	40	26	30	86	161	1	16	45	107	...	1	21	92	23	23	4
	ORDER 36.—TRADE IN BUILDING MATERIALS.																										
128	Trade in building materials (stones, bricks, plaster, cement, sand, tiles, thatch, etc.)...	571	135	35	4	...	401	1	21	14	4	3	15	34	1	5	6	13	4	...	6	6	13	6	5	11	2
	ORDER 37.—TRADE IN MEANS OF TRANSPORT.																										
129	Dealers and hirers of elephants, camels, horses, cattle, asses, mules, etc.; sellers (not makers) of carriages, saddlery, etc.	348	111	3	4	...	234	1	1	...	5	2	4	3	4	3	36	10	6	4	...	...	4	19	5	4	3
	ORDER 38.—TRADE IN FUEL.																										
130	Dealers in firewood, charcoal, coal, cowdung, etc.	2,827	786	357	13	...	1,684	22	72	95	70	43	24	105	187	32	92	49	37	40	8	17	50	80	87	95	18
	ORDER 39.—TRADE IN ARTICLES OF LUXURY AND THOSE PERTAINING TO LETTERS AND THE ARTS AND SCIENCES.																										
131	Dealers in precious stones, jewellery (real and imitation), clocks, optical instruments, etc.	3,115	992	40	12	...	2,063	4	44	12	46	77	60	230	263	78	13	48	23	20	1	5	16	40	37	8	7
132	Dealers in common bangles, bead neck-laces, fans, small articles, toys, hunting and fishing tackle, flowers, etc.	2,124	637	175	5	...	1,312	11	91	11	19	11	49	120	66	39	14	54	31	13	35	2	15	72	92	28	39
133	Publishers, book-sellers, stationers, dealers in music, pictures, musical instruments and curiosities	1,067	284	81	7	...	702	1	8	2	8	9	42	41	125	28	...	23	9	13	...	2	7	14	19	5	9

TABLE X.

Occupation—*continued.*

Group No.	DESCRIPTION OF OCCUPATION.	POPULATION SUPPORTED. Total workers and dependants.	Total actual workers. Males.	Total actual workers. Females.	Partially agriculturists. Males.	Partially agriculturists. Females.	Dependants.	ACTUAL WORKERS (BOTH SEXES) BY DIVISIONS. I.	II.	III.	IV.	V.	VI.	VII.	VIII.	IX.	X.	XI.	XII.	XIII.	XIV.	XV.	XVI.	XVII.	XVIII.	XIX.	XX.
1	2	3	4	5	6	7	8	9	10	11	12	13	14	15	16	17	18	19	20	21	22	23	24	25	26	27	28
	CLASS B.—PREPARATION AND SUPPLY OF MATERIAL SUBSTANCES—*cont.*																										
	ORDER 40.—TRADE IN REFUSE MATTER.																										
134	Dealers in rags, stable refuse, etc.	9	3	...	...	...	6	...	...	...	...	...	...	...	...	...	...	...	...	...	...	1	...	1	1	...	...
	ORDER 41.—TRADE OF OTHER SORTS.																										
135	Shopkeepers otherwise unspecified ...	5,703	1,721	104	42	...	3,878	28	57	12	197	195	96	156	210	73	34	242	44	78	22	63	65	75	69	60	54
136	Itinerant traders, pedlars, hawkers, etc. ...	987	305	44	1	...	638	...	10	...	5	5	9	9	22	80	...	48	108	13	...	6	7	16	7	4	...
137	Conjurors, acrobats, fortune tellers, reciters, exhibitors of curiosities and wild animals.	271	44	8	...	...	219	...	2	...	4	.	1	1	1	...	4	5	1	2	22	4	...	5	...	...	...
138	Other trades (including farmers of pounds, tolls and markets)	163	45	8	3	...	110		4	...	...	8	2	3	5	3	7	2	...	...	4	...	1	1	7	1	5
	CLASS C.—PUBLIC ADMINISTRATION AND LIBERAL ARTS.																										
	ORDER 42.—ARMY.																										
139	Army (Imperial)	2,415	1,077	...	3	...	1,338	1	4	4	13	3	554	8	11	10	11	12	112	36	28	7	58	124	18	55	8
140	Army (Native States)	2	2	...	...	...	...	...	...	...	...	1	...	.	...	...	...	...	...	...	...	...	...	...	...	...	1
	ORDER 44.—POLICE.*																										
142*	Police	6,190	1,902	3	48	...	4,285	32	117	39	28	68	90	114	72	69	89	126	124	226	8	61	114	159	115	191	63
143	Village watchmen	23	6	...	...	...	17	...	...	...	...	...	1	1	...	...	1	...	...	1	...	...	...	1	...	...	1
	ORDER 45.—PUBLIC ADMINISTRATION.																										
144	Service of the State	15,708	4,209	18	168	...	11,481	46	107	115	114	222	142	469	278	105	94	244	283	220	30	190	274	463	469	209	153
145	Service of Native and Foreign States ...	218	30	...	...	...	188	...	...	...	...	...	...	...	...	2	...	...	4	1	1	1	...	12	5	4	...
146	Municipal and other local (not village) service	7,963	2,695	74	32	...	5,194	33	245	90	29	84	95	156	353	50	242	364	107	173	39	39	96	104	89	324	57
147	Village officials and servants other than watchmen	205	55	2	3	...	148	1	7	3	2	...	4	2	1	1	7	...	...	3	1	2	...	2	6	8	7
	ORDER 46.—RELIGION.																										
148	Priests, ministers, etc.	2,396	802	17	52	...	1,577	16	24	15	22	65	57	92	119	54	5	37	18	13	6	16	11	64	86	32	67
149	Religious mendicants, inmates of monasteries, etc.	286	66	98	...	...	122	...	3	2	2	27	2	...	1	...	13	4	31	3	...	...	3	17	18	33	5

* No persons were returned under order 43 (group 141).

TABLE X.

Occupation—*continued.*

Group No.	DESCRIPTION OF OCCUPATION.	POPULATION SUPPORTED. Total workers and dependants.	Total actual workers. Males.	Total actual workers. Females.	Partially agriculturists. Males.	Partially agriculturists. Females.	Dependants.	ACTUAL WORKERS (BOTH SEXES) BY DIVISIONS. I.	II.	III.	IV.	V.	VI.	VII.	VIII.	IX.	X.	XI.	XII.	XIII.	XIV.	XV.	XVI.	XVII.	XVIII	XIX.	XX.
1	2	3	4	5	6	7	8	9	10	11	12	13	14	15	16	17	18	19	20	21	22	23	24	25	26	27	28
	CLASS C.—PUBLIC ADMINISTRATION AND LIBERAL ARTS—*cont.*																										
	ORDER 46.—RELIGION—*cont.*																										
150	Catechists, readers, church and mission service	1,078	188	66	2	...	824	12	13	4	5	11	11	8	6	...	5	50	42	8	15	19	18	3	10	6	8
151	Temple, burial or burning ground service, pilgrim conductors, circumcisers	1,827	647	69	17	...	1,111	7	42	28	19	29	40	42	77	70	9	57	19	16	3	10	24	47	80	53	44
	ORDER 47.—LAW.																										
152	Lawyers of all kinds, including Kazis, law agents and mukhtiars	2,140	381	...	50	...	1,759	3	10	4	24	35	8	21	21	15	...	7	28	31	8	7	6	18	40	21	74
153	Lawyers' clerks, petition writers, etc. ...	1,384	417	1	31	...	966	2	7	2	20	37	17	75	45	19	6	10	15	17	...	4	17	21	26	23	55
	ORDER 48.—MEDICINE.																										
154	Medical practitioners of all kinds, including dentists, oculists and veterinary surgeons.	4,724	1,196	73	39	...	3,455	38	79	27	33	61	67	126	79	67	19	107	65	53	21	28	61	125	86	79	48
155	Midwives, vaccinators, compounders, nurses, masseurs, etc.	2,295	576	441	14	...	1,278	43	110	12	8	37	41	52	47	103	16	37	90	143	22	26	64	52	40	65	9
	ORDER 49.—INSTRUCTION.																										
156	Professors and teachers of all kinds, and clerks and servants connected with education	8,283	2,110	737	87	1	5,436	93	126	56	66	150	125	223	110	31	61	260	224	121	42	112	108	297	285	187	170
	ORDER 50.—LETTERS AND ARTS AND SCIENCES.																										
157	Public scribes, stenographers, etc.	93	16	12	...	..	65	...	...	..	..	...	...	1	2	1	...	10	2	...	...	3	1	2	5	...	1
158	Architects, surveyors, engineers and their employés	5,094	1,465	9	53	...	3,620	30	35	15	51	30	46	107	47	20	28	23	70	76	17	41	74	272	296	132	64
159	Others (authors, photographers, artists, sculptors, astronomers, meteorologists, botanists, astrologers, etc.)	3,439	1,161	23	11	...	2,255	20	71	21	10	30	65	120	75	35	28	88	51	57	14	60	122	151	68	69	29
160	Music composers and masters, players on all kinds of musical instruments (not military), singers, actors and dancers ...	2,421	700	269	8	1	1,452	..	45	5	39	56	25	97	130	150	7	17	55	13	4	5	26	76	144	46	29
	ORDER 51.—PERSONS LIVING PRINCIPALLY ON THEIR INCOME.																										
161	Proprietors (other than of agricultural land), fund and scholarship holders and pensioners	19,855	4,385	2,176	128	28	13,294	146	425	237	176	273	310	533	379	311	495	509	421	280	30	140	328	448	635	263	222

TABLE X.

Occupation—*continued.*

Group No.	DESCRIPTION OF OCCUPATION.	POPULATION SUPPORTED.						ACTUAL WORKERS (BOTH SEXES) BY DIVISIONS.																			
		Total workers and dependants.	Total actual workers.		Partially agriculturists.		Dependants.	I.	II.	III.	IV.	V.	VI.	VII.	VIII.	IX.	X.	XI.	XII.	XIII.	XIV.	XV.	XVI.	XVII.	XVIII	XIX.	XX.
			Males.	Females.	Males.	Females.																					
1	2	3	4	5	6	7	8	9	10	11	12	13	14	15	16	17	18	19	20	21	22	23	24	25	26	27	28
	CLASS D.—MISCELLANEOUS.																										
	ORDER 52.—DOMESTIC SERVICE.																										
162	Cooks, water carriers, doorkeepers, watchmen and other indoor servants	26,849	7,810	5,597	74	2	13,242	479	366	102	490	598	579	678	840	457	198	940	1,164	866	765	1,029	601	639	688	1,129	799
163	Private grooms, coachmen, dog boys, etc. ...	7,979	2,663	153	7	..	5,163	46	63	20	86	94	200	164	148	65	34	97	212	182	194	277	112	310	117	228	167
	ORDER 53.—GENERAL TERMS WHICH DO NOT INDICATE A DEFINITE OCCUPATION.																										
164	Manufacturers, business men and contractors otherwise unspecified	2,056	531	9	23	...	1,516	14	18	14	21	34	27	64	21	20	12	94	27	16	7	4	37	22	34	48	6
165	Cashiers, accountants, book-keepers, clerks and other employés in unspecified offices, warehouses and shops	33,661	11,578	588	328	1	21,495	173	512	209	463	976	913	1,503	1,285	930	159	678	642	417	81	284	794	773	766	438	170
166	Mechanics otherwise unspecified	3,023	960	38	5	...	2,025	31	84	64	46	40	45	90	14	17	27	111	74	80	8	40	87	54	16	47	23
167	Labourers and workmen otherwise unspecified	26,571	8,721	4,113	19	2	13,737	317	1,138	321	605	614	920	507	495	443	681	1,067	1,037	544	431	680	1,031	739	366	723	176
	ORDER 54.—INMATES OF JAILS, ASYLUMS AND HOSPITALS.																										
168	Inmates of jails, asylums and hospitals ...	1,992	1,479	188	...	...	325	...	113	3	10	20	18	...	...	...	...	...	2	950	547	...	2	2	...	...	...
	ORDER 55.—BEGGARS, VAGRANTS AND PROSTITUTES.																										
169	Beggars, vagrants, procurers, prostitutes, receivers of stolen goods, cattle poisoners	5,339	1,295	2,045	3	12	1,999	27	193	102	83	208	94	480	738	227	127	144	61	73	53	38	93	184	201	113	101
	GRAND TOTAL ...	*518,660*	*164,427*	*35,884*	*2,134*	*70*	*318,349*	*7,492*	*17,208*	*6,052*	*6,452*	*7,375*	*9,704*	*13,473*	*12,111*	*7,895*	*9,657*	*16,005*	*10,864*	*9,274*	*5,426*	*5,470*	*9,471*	*13,476*	*12,085*	*12,842*	*7,979*

AGENTS FOR THE SALE OF MADRAS GOVERNMENT PUBLICATIONS.

IN INDIA.

R. Cambray & Co., Calcutta.
Combridge & Co., Madras.
T. Coopoosawmy Naiker & Co., Madras.
Higginbotham & Co., Mount Road, Madras.
V. Kalyanarama Iyer & Co., Esplanade, Madras.
G. C. Loganadham Brothers, Madras.
S. Murthy & Co., Kapalee Press, Madras.
G. A. Natesan & Co., Madras.
P. R. Rama Iyer & Co., Madras.
D. B. Taraporevala Sons & Co., Bombay.
Temple & Co., Georgetown, Madras.
Thacker & Co. (Limited), Bombay.
Thacker, Spink & Co., Calcutta.
Thompson & Co., Madras.

IN ENGLAND.

B. H. Blackwell, 50 and 51, Broad Street, Oxford.
Constable & Co., 10, Orange Street, Leicester Square, London, W.C.
Deighton, Bell & Co., Cambridge.
T. Fisher Unwin, 1, Adelphi Terrace, London, W.C.
Grindlay & Co., 54, Parliament Street, London, S.W.
Kegan Paul, Trench, Trübner & Co., 68–74, Carter Lane, London, E.C.
Henry S. King & Co., 65, Cornhill, London, E.C.
P. S. King & Son, 2 and 4, Great Smith Street, Westminster, London, S.W.
Luzac & Co., 46, Great Russell Street, London, W.C.
B. Quaritch, 11, Grafton Street, New Bond Street, London, W.
W. Thacker & Co., 2, Creed Lane, London, E.C.

ON THE CONTINENT.

Friedländer & Sohn, 11, Carlstrasse, Berlin.
Otto Harrassowitz, Leipzig.
Karl W. Hiersemann, Leipzig.
Ernest Leroux, 28, Rue Bonaparte, Paris.
Martinus Nijhoff, The Hague, Holland.